In A Flanders Field

John Waite

PEN & SWORD
HISTORY

First published in Great Britain in 2024 by
Pen & Sword History
An imprint of Pen & Sword Books Limited
Yorkshire – Philadelphia

ISBN 978 1 39903 723 5

A CIP catalogue record for this book is
available from the British Library

Typeset by Mac Style
Printed in the UK by CPI Group (UK) Ltd, Croydon, CR0 4YY.

Pen & Sword Books Limited incorporates the imprints of After
the Battle, Atlas, Archaeology, Aviation, Discovery, Family History,
Fiction, History, Maritime, Military, Military Classics, Politics,
Select, Transport, True Crime, Air World, Frontline Publishing, Leo
Cooper, Remember When, Seaforth Publishing, The Praetorian Press,
Wharncliffe Local History, Wharncliffe Transport, Wharncliffe True
Crime and White Owl.

For a complete list of Pen & Sword titles please contact

PEN & SWORD BOOKS LIMITED
47 Church Street, Barnsley, South Yorkshire, S70 2AS, England
E-mail: enquiries@pen-and-sword.co.uk
Website: www.pen-and-sword.co.uk
or
PEN AND SWORD BOOKS
1950 Lawrence Rd, Havertown, PA 19083, USA
E-mail: Uspen-and-sword@casematepublishers.com
Website: www.penandswordbooks.com

In A Flanders Field

This book is dedicated to the memory of my Great Uncle and hero, Joseph James Waite, MM and all of his comrades from the 1/7th (TF) Bn, The Royal Warwickshire Regiment. Especially all of those men of the battalion who, after four years of fighting, never came home.

LEST WE FORGET

"Politicians who took us to war should have been given the guns and told to settle their differences themselves, instead of organising nothing better than legalised mass murder."

Harry Patch, the Last Fighting Tommy

Contents

Acknowledgements

There is always a fear, when attempting to acknowledge all the help and support that has gone into making a book happen, that you will miss somebody. Though, in all honesty, there have been so many contributions in the more than seven years it has taken to write this book that even I wouldn't be able to recall them all. Therefore, even though a name or organisation might not be listed here, I just want everybody involved to know that I am sincerely grateful for their input.

As a starting point, I must say a huge thank you to my family, both past and present. If not for their numerous contributions, I would have had no starting point to work from and none of the anecdotal or photographic material that they provided me with. Nor too do I overlook the fact that I could have only achieved completion of this book with the patience and understanding of my wife, Helen, who has supported me throughout the years it has taken to complete this work. From sitting alone on many a night while I worked, to joining me on visits to memorials, museums and even the battlefields of Ypres themselves, she has been with me all the way. So too has she understood just how much it means to me to be able to tell the stories you are about to read.

I am profoundly grateful to the many veterans, both inside and outside the family, who either directly, or in third-party form, shared their knowledge and experiences, thus enabling me to develop some understanding of what they went through. My gratitude also extends to a number of churches that have graciously allowed me access in order to photograph and record details of just a few of the many memorials that commemorate those men remembered in this work. In that regard, I must make special mention of Mark Phillips of Albion Archaeology, who was kind enough to photograph for me the memorial in St Mary's Church, Bedford and then most graciously grant permission for its inclusion in this work. Some years ago, the church was converted to commercial use and is no longer accessible to the public. Therefore, a man on the inside was invaluable.

In terms of filling in gaps and providing special nuggets of information, I must first thank David Baynham of the Royal Regiment of Fusiliers Museum at Warwick. His encyclopaedic knowledge of the history of the Royal Warwickshire Regiment and where to look for those nuggets helped my early research so much and allowed me to develop my own skills in that area.

Providing some phenomenally valuable nuggets too was my good friend, Nath Houghton. Nath is the great nephew of Corporal Arthur Hutt VC, about whom you will read more of later, and during the course of his own research, he uncovered a number of absolutely invaluable facts about my uncle Joe. These really did allow me to develop a much fuller picture of Joe's life, both as a boy and later in life. I therefore cannot thank Nath enough. Not only did he provide me with great research material, his work also allowed me to form a greater understanding of my own family history.

In April 2017, nearly 100 years after the battle, I visited Ypres and the Flanders region with my wife and youngest son, Marcus. I therefore must mention Patrick from 2explore Flanders Fields, a Belgian company that specialise in tours of the local battlefields. His amazing local knowledge and the effort he put into preparing for our visit not only ensured that I developed a greater understanding of the events of October 1917. He also ensured that I set foot on the very same ground that those brave lads fought for, more than a century ago. To stand next to the very spot where Tweed House stood and survey that ground was, I can assure you, a truly unforgettable experience and one I will be forever grateful to Patrick for arranging.

It's a sad fact that very few of the soldiers in this book have photographs to accompany their stories. However, in one instance, I was not only provided photos but also a significant amount of background history by Nicola Waddington, the archivist at Alleyn's School, Dulwich. The material and photographs she provided me with, combined with the consent to publish the material, were invaluable in being able to tell the story of Private Cecil Core.

I am also grateful for the assistance given by another educational establishment, Bristol Grammar School, for their help in piecing together the story of Captain John Croall. Their archivist, Anne Bradley, was kind enough to send not only information about John, but also photographs from a recent school trip to Tyne Cot, where poppies were laid in his memory.

During the course of my research, I discovered that the name of Lance Corporal William Treadgold had been omitted from a local war memorial, which should have borne his name. However, once I had flagged this up to Rugby Borough Council, Chris Worman MBE, the council's Parks and Grounds Manager, took the matter in hand. His hard work liaising with the monument owners, a developer called St Modwen, the Royal Warwickshire Regiment and the Ministry of Defence ensured that William's name was subsequently added to the memorial, thus ensuring that he can now be remembered publicly as well as by his family.

Thanks must also go to a number of family members of the soldiers I have written about. Both for the responses I have had from them and for their good wishes for getting the book published. I am also very grateful for the kind consent, where granted, to use some of the limited numbers of photos I have found of the men. For the photos of those soldiers whose families are not credited, I must point out that every effort was made to contact them and to seek permission to use the images of their relatives, even though the images exist in the public domain. This last was particularly important to me as I wanted the families of as many of these men as possible to know that their sacrifice was going to be acknowledged in this work.

Beyond what I have genuinely understood to be public domain material, I have made every reasonable effort to correctly credit images and ascertain, locate and contact copyright holders. However, it has taken me more than seven years to gather material for this book and many of the photos are now well over a century old and drawn from many sources. I am therefore conscious that it may prove that some photos may not have been correctly attributed. If such is the case, any error in that regard is entirely my own and totally unintentional.

Essentially, every attempt has been made to ascertain, locate and contact potential copyright holders of the images used. However, I would ask that any copyright holders that believe their material has been incorrectly attributed or credited, make themselves known to the publishers so that they may be fully credited and acknowledged in any future reprint of this book.

At the start of this project, my technical knowledge of the Great War was fairly basic. Over the time taken to write this book, it has since grown considerably in relation to the fighting on the Western Front. That said, I never would have been able to either understand or interpret some of the information I had gathered had it not been for a group of people whose specialist knowledge of the period was almost available 'on tap'. I refer of course to the members of an online resource, 'The Great War Forum', which I genuinely believe to be an absolutely invaluable resource.

To be able to go onto the forum, ask a question and receive an almost instantaneous answer was such a boon to my research. Consequently, while I am not able to remember the names of all of those members who rendered me such expert assistance, I would nevertheless like to extend my most sincere thanks to those members who so patiently shared their knowledge with me.

Lastly, I must say a huge thank you to Sarah-Beth Watkins, Senior Commissioning Editor for history at Pen & Sword Books Ltd. I genuinely do believe that fate conspired to grant me the publishing contract that subsequently arose from a chance email. To her, I am so very grateful that by her faith in my proposal and her subsequent efforts on my behalf, this book became a reality and that the story of Joe and his fallen comrades can now be told to a wider audience.

John Waite, 21 March 2023. Coventry

In Flanders Fields

In Flanders fields the poppies blow
Between the crosses, row on row,
That mark our place; and in the sky
The larks, still bravely singing, fly
Scarce heard amid the guns below.

We are the Dead. Short days ago
We lived, felt dawn, saw sunset glow,
Loved and were loved, and now we lie,
In Flanders fields.

Take up our quarrel with the foe:
To you from failing hands we throw
The torch; be yours to hold it high.
If ye break faith with us who die
We shall not sleep, though poppies grow
In Flanders fields.

Major John McCrae
Canadian Expeditionary Force, May 1915

Introduction

The first thing that I should make clear is the fact that this book has been written, not as any sort of battalion history, but as a unique biographical tribute. That said, this is not a typical biography either. Though the work will broadly capture the life story of my great uncle, Joe Waite, it is also intended to stand as a dedicated act of remembrance for another sixty-four Great War soldiers.

It is a never-ending source of pride to me that Joe's incredible bravery, just outside the Belgian city of Ypres, on 4 October 1917, saw him awarded the Military Medal (MM). Though, as I've grown older and I've learnt more about the Great War, it has often made me pause for thought. As my understanding of the nature of the fighting grew and how men were killed on an industrial scale, I began to think in much more depth about the men who did not come home.

In our family, as with so many others, remembrance of our war dead is regarded as a solemn and ongoing duty. Every year, we make our donations, wear our poppies with pride and parade alongside our comrades from the various services we served in, or still serve in. But, as I've already said, in recent years my attention turned not just to memorials, both grand and modest, but to the stories of ordinary servicemen. Not those famous generals, or other well-known names from history whose stories are still told today, but the unknowns.

Of course, over the years, film and social media have shared the stories of many ordinary people from the Great War. A host of documentaries, books and films have told us the stories, not just of veterans of the services, but of those on the home front too. But these are mostly stories of those who survived – able to sit in front of a camera or biographer and share their story. Also true is the fact that these are largely the stories of individuals and not that of larger, linked groups of people.

And what of those who didn't survive? They who sacrificed everything and could not tell their own stories. Those whose names, many of which are now lost to time. Their stories deserve telling too, but the chance to tell them to a wider audience is so often missed. Clearly, the ability to tell all of those countless untold stories is not an option. However, with time, diligence and patience, the chance to shed light on the lives of men from just one unit, at one place in time is still possible.

For me, that chance presented itself when, in early 2017, I became involved in organising the one-hundredth anniversary commemoration of Corporal Arthur Hutt's award of the Victoria Cross (VC). Arthur is so far the only person born in my home town of Coventry to have received Britain's highest award for bravery in battle. The story of Arthur's heroic acts that day is linked to that of my uncle Joe as both he and Arthur were part of the same battalion. Both men, as with their comrades, fought hard to achieve their objectives that day, among some of the worst conditions the Western Front had yet to offer.

I'd already built up a pretty good picture of what went on that day from years of researching Joe's story. I'd even started work the previous year on writing Joe's story. But then it occurred to me that I had missed something. That 'something' was the stories of those men from Joe and Arthur's unit who had also gone into battle around that time but who had not come home. From that point on, I resolved that I would tell at least something of the stories of each of those men of the battalion who lost their lives in battle during the month of October 1917, and in particular, during the Battle of Broodseinde, fought between 4 – 7 October.

It's reasonable, I think, to assume that most authors would want their readers to finish their book feeling as though they had come across something just a little bit different. That the experience was actually a satisfying change to anything else they may have read. Certainly, in respect of my own previous non-fiction offerings, the desire to produce books that stepped away from the norm was always a key driver for me. And yet, with this work, it was nothing less than essential for me to feel that I had achieved that.

A good start then, for me to have accepted my own challenge by moving completely away from my normal subject matter and more traditional reference sources, such as specialist books and publications. Instead, this book avoids that norm, opting instead for largely Internet-based sources. Anything from Government and organisational websites, to online genealogical resources. Or the use of official online archives and locally compiled pages, recording local men, histories or memorials. Because of this, the need to accompany my work with a traditional bibliography did not arise. Instead, I have listed elsewhere, a select compilation of some of the sites and sources used in order to complete this book.

As somebody who was born in the early 1960s, I, like all of my generation, had the immense privilege of growing up with the veterans of the Great War still all around us. As a Coventry kid, I also lived with almost daily stories of how my city made its mark in both world wars. On occasion, I heard too the accounts of those who returned from those conflicts. I also grew to learn and understand the pain and grief of the families left behind. Either for the loss of the men who did not come home, or for those killed on the home front in the very city I was growing up in. For those survivors, deep scars still remained. Although, from a very early age, I recognised that the veterans of the Great War were different. Men like Old Man Greer from across the back jetty (that's what old Coventry folk call an alley) who, every day, used to come shuffling down to the back garden gate on his walking frame. Puffing away on a Woodbine and carrying the experience of well over ninety years on earth with an easy dignity, he would, in his growling but good-natured voice, ask me the usual question:

'What you up to today then, young un?'

Even at my young age, he fascinated me, telling me about life in the British Army of yesteryear. He had served as a professional soldier with the Royal Warwickshire Regiment (Royal Warwicks), first in the Second Boer War and then in India, before he eventually returned homeward to become embroiled in the first global conflict in history. His experience was, even at that time, an increasingly rare first-hand account of a dramatic shift in how war was fought. His was a story of somebody who had witnessed the transformation of combat from the conflicts of the late Victorian period, through into the early twentieth century. He understood what the advent of a war driven by killing on an industrial scale actually meant. Not least because he had been able to compare and contrast old wars and war on a brutally epic scale. Yet, for all of that, there was never any real detail that he cared to impart about what he saw or did. It was always more about the lads he served with, life in camp, or the funny things that happened.

As he was an old Royal Warwick, to my delight, he once let me borrow his sizeable collection of *The Antelope*, the old regimental magazine. How well I remember them, dog-eared and brown with age, smelling just like old print should. They were full of photographs of the 'Warwicks' in Peshawar, where his battalion was based around 1912. I didn't really understand them too much, of course. After all, I was far too young then. But, oh, how I wish now that I could look at them just once more.

If I wanted to hear talk of fighting, I generally had to get it third-hand and ask relatives. Even then, there was little on offer, because he seldom spoke about it to anyone. In fact, the only thing I really learned about his time in actual combat was the story he told of being posted as a trench guard, left behind to challenge any men who ran back to British positions as an assault went forward. All Old Man Greer would tell anyone was that soon after his unit went over the top that day, a young Irish lad came running back to the trench, utterly terrified. Greer did no more than thrust his rifle, with bayonet fixed, towards the poor lad. He then told him, very bluntly, to get back over there, or he'd shoot him. He apparently always supported that story with a very firm:

'And I bloody well would have, you know!'

To be honest, I don't think anyone who knew him ever doubted that he would have followed up the threat. Though ultimately, it transpires that he didn't have the need to, as he finished the story by confirming that the frightened young soldier reluctantly turned back towards the fighting and was never seen again.

However, for all that I was very taken by Old Man Greer's engaging and affable nature, there was one other old Royal Warwick who will always be my favourite veteran of the Great War. That man is Joe Waite, my maternal great-uncle, and my absolute hero.

Though it would take many years of research and discovery, my understanding of Joe and what transpired to be his often-difficult life would finally evolve into the picture I have of him today. I adored the old man who used to fall asleep in front of the TV whilst watching 'World of Sport' on a Saturday afternoon. He never really minded that much that I used to play spiders on his bald spot, either. Full of mischief and giggling under my breath, I would sneak up and scrabble my fingers over his head from behind the back of the armchair. Inevitably, as was the intention, the intrusion would wake him with a start and he'd then make a bit of noise about it himself. Usually firing off something in the order of:

'Gerrout of it, you little bugger. I'm having a kip!'

That was usually my cue to run off into the back room, laughing that I had got a bite out of him. Joe, for his part, normally settled back down again, plumped his cushion up and nodded back off with a half-smile on his face.

Joe did have a bit of an aptitude for getting into trouble though. One day, he took me to the local pub, The King's Head, on Blackberry Lane, and set me down outside with a bottle of pop and a bag of crisps. Unfortunately for Joe, whilst he was inside the pub having a drink, curiosity got the better of me and I ran out into the nearby road – God knows why. Anyway, I never actually achieved whatever it was I'd set out to do. Instead, I got run over by the local police car. Joe didn't half get into trouble for that one, I can tell you!

According to my nan, Maggie Waite, Joe and my grandad – his brother, George – were as different as chalk and cheese. Grandad, although younger than Joe, died a few years before him. He was much more the family man by all accounts. A good deal more placid by nature than Joe and very dependable. Certainly, I remember a kind and gentle man who, though I was only very young, loved to teach me about Coventry's rich heritage. Even today, I can visit sites in the city, such as the Old Cathedral, St Mary's Hall, Cook Street Gate and Ford's Hospital to name but a few and still see him in my mind's eye, telling me their names and how old they were, it is to that lovely, thoughtful man that I owe my love of history and when 'Papap' died, the crowd that turned out for his funeral left no doubt in anyone's mind that George Waite was a man held in high regard by a lot of people.

Joe, however, was apparently a bit of a hot head. Indeed, both my nan and mum, Judy, would tell me that he had to go around the family on more than one occasion to apologise for behaviour such as getting into fights and thus bringing the family name into disrepute.

As though to validate that assessment of his character, an article from a local newspaper in September 1939, seems to suggest that this critique of Joe's personality may not have been too wide of the mark. It read that Joe had been issued with a summons to appear at Lichfield Magistrates on a charge of driving without due care and attention. Apparently, in the previous August, Joe had been riding a motorbike and side-car combination along the Chester Road, between Brownhills and Birmingham, when he had jumped a red light and collided with a coach crossing the Shire Oak crossroads. It seems that Joe had declined to attend the court in person and had instead telephoned to make his apologies and offer some defence for his actions. Apparently, in mitigation, Joe claimed that one of the signals at the junction was not working. He had then been overtaken by a speeding car at the moment of approaching the junction and could not see the working light. However, despite both a witness and PC Mutter, the police officer in court confirming these facts, the case against Joe was proven and he was fined £1, with £2.13/10d (2 pounds, 13 shillings and 10 pence) to be paid as costs. Whether my family ever got to hear of this, I can't say. What I do know is that it would certainly not have gone down well if they had.

As I shall recount later on, Joe's demeanour later in life may have been partially attributable to tragic events unfolding long after his service in the Great War. Though, my ability to better understand his war service was not actually gained by whatever he told me, or many others for that matter. Rather, it was my nan who turned out to be the chief source of much of the knowledge that formed the bones of what I later discovered about him.

Just as a detective chases down leads, Nan provided me with a number of lines of enquiry. All I had to do was keep my childhood curiosity alive, apply skills learned in my subsequent career choices and become the recipient of some occasional good fortune in order to exploit those leads.

In the first years of my life, I lived with my mum at Nan and Grandad's house and it was not long after Papap died that Joe came to live with us for a while. I'm sure, having been his sister-in-law for many years, Nan had learned a lot about Joe, but she didn't really begin to tell me much about him until after he too had passed away. Nan told me a lot about life on the home front in the Coventry of World War Two. Also, a little bit about my grandad's role in the Home Guard and her experiences too. Particularly on the night of the Coventry Blitz. But she also talked about Joe's army service. I think this was because, in her own way, she was very proud of what Joe had done too. She explained that he had lied about his age and joined up at 16. She also said he mentioned a gruesome story about jumping into a trench and landing on the chest of a dead German, whose tongue had promptly popped out. Intriguingly, she also mentioned the fact that she thought he had won a medal for knocking out a German machine gun. Albeit, she didn't know where. I wasn't to know it at the time, but this last nugget would be a vital link into the story I will come to tell as it proved ultimately to be true.

Perhaps the saddest thing to have arisen from the knowledge that Joe was indeed awarded a gallantry medal, a Military Medal (MM) in fact, is that we no longer have either that medal, or the campaign medals that accompanied it. Although I commissioned a duplicate set some years ago, the originals have long since disappeared. From what my mother tells me, it is most likely to have been after Joe had handed the medals to my grandad for safe-keeping in the mid to late 1960s. The story goes that they were put in a set of drawers that were later tidied out, with the medals being mistakenly thrown out with rubbish from the drawers. Joe was understandably very upset at their loss and initially accused my nan of selling them, which was something she always steadfastly denied. Obviously, it caused a major row in the family. But beyond that, I have never been able to understand why he thought this.

To this day, I simply cannot answer the question of why somebody who so clearly respected what Joe had done, would hurt him in that way? Perhaps Joe's accusation was born purely of the upset that he felt at losing things that must have been so very precious to him. Either way, the explanation that the medals were lost as a result of carelessness during the clean-out of those drawers makes far more sense to me.

Ultimately, whether the medals ended up at Coventry tip or were rescued by somebody is never likely to be known. Though, if by some astonishing twist

Replica set of Joe Waite's medals. (*Author's photo*)

of fate, the medals were saved from destruction, perchance, the current keeper might read this book and contact me to negotiate their return? A long shot, I know. But I live in hope.

Though Uncle Joe lived until I was about 9 years old, I never got to ask him about the war. In those days you see, it wasn't really appropriate for children so young to ask such things. And so, ultimately, all I had left to remember him by were my childhood memories and an old photo of him in uniform, proudly wearing his medals. Though I never knew it then, that photo would eventually become the key that would lead me to the knowledge I now have. Eventually I would come to learn of such things such as the circumstances behind his decision to enlist, the places where he fought and about the men who fought next to him.

Ultimately, Joe's story provided me with a great moment of pride. As I've mentioned, I eventually established that he had been awarded an MM. Even more significantly for me, as a proud Coventrian, was that it was for bravery during the same action that led to the only Victoria Cross (VC) so far being awarded to a Coventry-born serviceman, Corporal Arthur Hutt. My amazing Uncle Joe, I discovered, had fought alongside Arthur at the Battle of Passchendaele. That created what I saw as an astounding family connection to a feat of heroism that, even today, is still a tremendous source of pride to the city.

Portrait of Lance Corporal 265951 Joe Waite. Given that he is wearing all of his campaign medals, the photo is likely to have been taken after the battalion returned home and prior to 'de-mob'. The medals are, from left to right: Military Medal, 1914-15 Star, British War Medal and Victory Medal. (*Waite family archive*)

Though, even as I savoured the sense of awe I felt for my own family hero, my mind was already turning towards thoughts of the other soldiers who had fought alongside Joe and Arthur on a distant Belgian battlefield. More especially, I began to consider just how many of them had not survived the action. Here was I, full of pride at my own relative's achievements and the fact that I had been gifted with the immense privilege of knowing him. And yet, I knew there would be many families who, for the sake of that one action, would never have been able to experience what I had. They had never been given the opportunity to meet their own family member, because he had instead fallen during the fighting. It was that realisation that created in me an intense resolve to learn as much as I could about these men too.

As a research project, it was lengthy and oftentimes quite harrowing. That said, it was also incredibly rewarding. Only by taking on this task could I have developed any understanding of the cost of sending just one infantry battalion to fight in a three-day battle that formed a small part of a much larger campaign. Indeed, it is a battle within a battle, that anybody who is unfamiliar with the various campaigns of the Western Front would probably never have heard of.

As I was drawn ever deeper into my research, I discovered stories of men who were determined to fight for king and country. They achieved it by whatever means necessary. Some by lying about their age – just as Joe had. And even in one notable example by travelling many thousands of miles, just to be able to enlist. I learned too of the families left behind and discovered the outpourings of pain as they struggled with their grief. So too had I learned the stories of men who had won their own gallantry medals, though some posthumously, never to know how proud their families were of what they had done.

Researching these men meant learning about so many ways to feel the sorrow of the bereaved – children left fatherless, a sweetheart or young wife left devastated. Even parents robbed not just of one son, but eventually of every boy they had. Where graves existed, there would sometimes be a few touching words inscribed on the stone to convey the thoughts of those left behind. And yet, in so many cases, I found that the bodies of their menfolk had no known grave. Some may have initially been laid to rest in any number of battlefield cemeteries. However, this was no guarantee of a permanent resting place. Very often, repeated shelling churned up the ground in which they had been laid to rest, destroying their grave markers and dooming their mortal remains to anonymity as a final indignity. The stark reality is that the terrible power of

The headstone of an unknown soldier of the Royal Warwickshire Regiment. Tyne Cot cemetery. (*Author's photo*)

modern weaponry meant that fragile human bodies became so badly shattered that they were most often rendered unidentifiable. Worse still, in so many instances, their mortal remains had simply disappeared. The awful power of the guns on this terrible new battlefield could quite literally vapourise a man, almost making it seem as though he had never existed.

It got to the point that I could not stop my research, even if I had wanted to. Night after night, I would return from work and begin to trawl again through so many sources, desperate almost to be able to tell at least a little something about each one of the names I had identified. These were the men who fell in October 1917. Either in the three days of the battle itself, or in the days following the fighting and before the battalion was moved from the immediate area of the front. For me, it was almost as if I was now honour-bound to uncover details of the lives of men who Joe may have known as comrades, or even whose sacrifice may have helped him to live through the hell of that battle. Somehow, I felt as though I owed them that.

For some of those men, death would not claim them in the midst of actual combat. A few would have fallen victim to any number of hazards located close to the front. There were those too who, having been wounded in battle, would have succumbed to their wounds. Like so many others, their lives would have slipped away in any number of forward dressing stations, casualty clearing stations and field hospitals serving the area. All of them were men who Joe may well have known in some way or other. He'd spent time with them. He'd experienced things alongside them that most of us could never imagine. He'd seen some of them fall.

As will become apparent, this is a book with a difference. Not so much a standard biography of one man's war, so much as it is his story, told alongside others who also deserve to have their lives celebrated. As you will later read, I have come to be able to tell quite detailed stories of some of these men. Yet, sadly, there are also those where I have been able to add very little at all. But, for the latter, I have at least been able to say just a little something beyond the brief summaries contained within the records of the Ministry of Defence (MOD) and Commonwealth War Graves Commission (CWGC).

For me though, the most precious discoveries of all are the photos. Just very occasionally during my searching, I would let out a 'whoop' of joy as I punched the air in triumph. Rarely did it happen but there before me would be the face of a soldier, looking out at me from behind the shadows of more than a century. To some, just a photograph. But to me, each one was a priceless reflection of men to whom the world owes a debt that can never be settled. As with the personal stories of the men themselves, these photos underpin the fact that it was not just young men who fell, but older ones too. The faces of young lads can be found here. But so too can those of older men. All are testament to the indiscriminate nature of their deaths and the void they left behind for their loved ones.

At this point, I think it is an opportune moment to ease back a little and underline some further decision-making on my part. The fact is, this book is not intended to be any sort of definitive account of Joe's unit, or a detailed history of its part in the war on the Western Front. Neither is it meant to be a fully referenced account of the particular period that this work ultimately relates to.

Of course, I appreciate that the above omissions in this work may disappoint the more academic or technical reader. However, it is quite a deliberate decision on my part, made to ensure that the book appeals to as wide an audience as possible. Moreover, I have also elected not to go into any great detail relating to the German forces they faced, or the specific positions the enemy held. This is all information that can be found elsewhere. Because, in my opinion, adding too much here would only take the focus off the stories of the men to whom this book is ultimately dedicated.

In the pages that follow, I will tell you more about Joe Waite. After all, he is where the story starts and the account of his upbringing as a tough, working-class Coventry lad is key to understanding how he grew to become the man he was. As you will come to appreciate, his is a story of hardship, heroism and great personal tragedy, and is one that should be told. Though, as I have already said, the story of the fallen is also of the utmost importance here. This is a unique opportunity to celebrate collectively the lives they left behind. So too is it a testament to their service and finally to the ultimate sacrifice they made in battle. Where I can, I will tell too of how their families and communities remembered them. But ultimately, the gathering and sharing of all this information has just one aim:

To celebrate the lives and memory of those men of the 1/7 Battalion (Bn), the Royal Warwickshire Regiment, who fought and fell around the time of the Battle of Broodseinde. A little-known action, fought in blood-soaked fields of mud near the Belgian city of Ypres in October 1917.

Chapter 1
From Cradle to Khaki

Born in the Foleshill district of Coventry on 22 August 1898, Joseph James Waite was the first of five children born to Joseph, an engineering worker, and Matilda (nee Hazlewood). The first of his siblings, William Frederick, was born in October 1890. Though William did not live for long and passed away the December after he was born. He was followed by Ethel, who was born on 16 October 1902; by Laura, on 23 June 1904, and lastly by George, on 5 October 1906.

Joe's birth came just as the Victorian era was coming to an end. Living in the heart of one of Britain's great industrial cities, his upbringing was typical for a working-class child growing up at the time. Around the turn of the century, industrial production in Coventry was geared towards the manufacture of engineered goods and the city was filled not only with vast factories and workshops large and small, but also large areas of the very basic housing needed to accommodate the workers. Located mostly in the northwest quarter and central areas of Coventry, these very densely populated areas were often situated right next to the factories they served. As such, Joe's entire childhood was spent in those areas.

Working in manufacturing was in Joe's blood. Not only was his father a second-generation engineering worker, but his mother, Matilda, was a

James Washington Hazlewood.
(*Waite family archive*)

Hazlewood by birth. Hailing variously from the areas of South Warwickshire and North Oxfordshire, members of the Hazlewood family had moved to the city around the mid-1800s. As with many of the Hazlewoods who left their home villages, Matilda's grandfather, Samuel, was a blacksmith. He had carried on with his trade after moving from the South Warwickshire village of Knighton, to Coventry with his wife, Mary Ann Woolford. It was their son, James Washington Hazlewood, also a blacksmith, who subsequently married Mary Ann

Joe Waite Snr.
(*Waite family archive*)

Davitt in Coventry on 22 December 1878. Their first child, Matilda, was then born in Coventry in July 1879.

It was another James Hazlewood, hailing from Hanwell in Oxfordshire and believed to be a cousin, who diversified into manufacturing and first established a bicycle manufacturing workshop, The Hazlewood Cycle Company, in the Bishopsgate Green area of Coventry in 1876. The business grew well over the years and later moved to larger premises at West Orchards and began to produce motorcycles from around 1911, trading this time as Hazlewoods Limited. However, neither Samuel nor Matilda's father, James, were thought to have had any direct connection with that business.

Young Joe himself was the third in succession of his line to be called Joseph Waite. His grandfather, the oldest Joseph, was an engine fitter and was born in Huddersfield, Yorkshire around 1835. He married Hannah Moore at Newark

Register Office, Nottinghamshire, on 24 January 1865. Young Joe's father, another Joseph, was born in Birmingham in the second quarter of 1878 and was one of eight children born to the couple. It is not known when the Waites first moved to Coventry from Birmingham, but they are shown as living in Jordan Well, in the city centre, by the time of the 1891 census. His branch of the family started in 1898 when he married Matilda, who then gave birth to young Joe in the same year.

By the time of the 1901 census, the young family, numbering just three at that point, were living at 490, Stoney Stanton Road. This was close to an area of Foleshill, which is ironically referred to as Paradise. In those days, it was close to several large factories and smaller workshops, which would have filled the air with all manner of very unpleasant emissions. Paradise, it certainly was not. Certainly, even as a child, I remember growing up not far from the Morris Engines factory and foundry and I can still remember the acrid smell and thick smog that regularly filled the air – even in the mid-1960s.

Though it is unknown when, the family subsequently moved to 7, Steam Yard, in East Street. This was located closer to the city centre, in the Hillfields area of the city. At the time, a good proportion of the housing close to the centre of the city was turned over to poor-quality accommodation called 'courts'. These were essentially slum tenements that usually shared small open spaces, often with just one hand pump for water and with only very basic sanitation. All of which were shared by a number of dwellings. At best, they were cramped two-up, two-down houses. Though, at worst, they were just a few small rooms, offering neither adequate privacy nor space for their occupants.

Often, the life people lived in them was only a step or two up from a bed in the workhouse. Nevertheless, as with every other major town or city, this was where the lowest-paid workers in the city lived, cheek by jowl, but thankful enough that they had the means to pay their way and live by their own, often meagre means. Still, life carried on in the little two-up, two-down house in Steam Yard and the Waite family, as with their neighbours, got on with living the only life they knew.

In 1909, the Waites were typical of many of the working-class families in the area. By then young Joe was around 11 years old and big brother to 2-year-old George – my grandad, and Ethel and Laura, who were 7 and 5 years old, respectively. There to look after them all was their mother, Matilda. She was the glue that bound them all together and at the end of that year, she was pregnant once more. As such, all of them must have been eagerly awaiting the birth of their new baby brother or sister. Though, only days after the family had celebrated Christmas, an awful tragedy struck.

On 30 December, Matilda died during childbirth. She was just 30 years old and had developed Placenta Previa Flooding. This is a birth complication that essentially means that the unborn baby's placenta blocks the neck of the womb, catastrophically obstructing the child's birth if not quickly acted upon. Though the complication is less problematic to treat today, in 1909 it would have proven fatal to any mother and infant not fortunate enough to be receiving immediate and skilled medical attention. And so, just before the new year, both Matilda and the unborn child died in the most heartbreaking of circumstances. As a consequence, the young family were thrown into the midst of not only grief but serious turmoil.

An early photo of Matilda Waite, nee Hazlewood. (*Waite family archive*)

It is impossible to even begin to understand the utter shock and numbness that Joe Snr must have felt. Less than a week before, they had all celebrated Christmas as a family. Now, Matilda, the cornerstone of their world, had gone. As for the children – at two years old, my grandad, George, would have had little comprehension of what was happening. However, the pain of losing their mum would have been very real for Joe and his sisters. Though much worse was to come, as their father would have quickly realised that he would never be able to work and take care of them all.

Even though it essentially amounted to a life of drudgery, a woman's role in any working-class family of the time was vital. She was the one who ran the house and did all of the jobs that needed doing in order to keep them all going. Her never-ending cycle of chores ensured that the children were properly looked after, clothed, fed and schooled. She also shopped and cleaned and generally made sure that the man of the house was unburdened by the majority of day-to-day domestic tasks and thereby free to earn the money that paid for it all. With the loss of Matilda, none of this was possible for a new widower on his own. And so, as all those around him turned to celebrating the turn of a new decade, Joe Snr had to face up to an awful truth. Not only had his wife been cruelly taken from him, but his family would also have to be split up.

Joe's own parents were not an option in terms of caring for the children. His mother, Hannah, had died in 1896 and his father was by then around 76 years old and living a very impoverished existence in the courts at Cow Lane, in the city centre. And so it was then, that the two Joes remained at Steam Yard, while little George and the girls were sent to live with Grandma Hazlewood who, at that time, was living in rooms at the rear of 44, Spon Street.

Matilda's mother, Mary Ann Hazlewood, was by the time of the 1911 Census, a 56-year-old widow. Her husband, James, had died the previous year. By way of a measure of how poor the family were, his father, Samuel, had previously been admitted to the Coventry Union Workhouse on 9 June 1906. He passed away in the workhouse infirmary on 22 August of the same year. The notes from the discharge book state that he was receiving a diet suited to the 'infirm' and that he was considered to be 'destitute'.

As well as the three grandchildren she had taken in, Mary Ann was working at home and also housing her two adult sons: James, a 29-year-old turner, and Frederick, 26, a blacksmith's stoker. There were also two daughters: Helena, a 23-year-old press hand, and Winnifred, 19, who was working as an examiner for a cycle chain factory. Present also was May, 24, James's wife, and their daughter, three-year-old Ethel May. As the youngest of the Waite children, George remained at home. However, Ethel and Laura were attending day

A view down Spon Street, Coventry. Taken during the flooding of 1900, the tower of St John's Church can be seen at the end of the street. The Hazlewoods would have lived in rooms to the rear of the buildings on the right of the street. (*Author's collection*)

school at the local church, St John's, which was a stone's throw away at the end of Spon Street. Nevertheless, even though most of the adults were working, the best they could afford was a living space comprising just one large living room and two bedrooms.

By today's standards, it is extremely hard to even begin to imagine how so many people were able to co-exist with each other in such cramped conditions. Yet, these were people of their time and what we would see as fairly well impossible to cope with these days, was instead a situation they simply had to make the best of. As such, they just knuckled down and did what it took to get through. After all, their circumstances were by no means extraordinary for the period. Consequently, it was against this background that the young Waite family carried on as best they could and ultimately how, as events began to unfold, that big brother Joe eventually came to enlist.

The 1911 Census also confirms that young Joe and his father were still residing at 7, Steam Yard. However, living with them by then was James Davitt, a 48-year-old labourer. The surname Davitt is also the maiden name of Joe's grandmother Mary Ann Hazlewood, wife of James. Consequently, some form of familial connection existed but still requires a little more research.

At the time of the census, young Joe was recorded as being 13, and his father 33 and working for Daimler at their vast Radford plant. Though, the information collected on the census form itself is quite basic. There is, therefore, no information currently available to understand just what the actual nature of the relationship was between James and the two Joes. Curiously though, the record does show that James had listed himself as head of the household and that Joe Senior was actually listed as his son. Yet, even by virtue of their relative ages, this was clearly not an accurate declaration. In fairness to James though, it is clear from the standard of handwriting and spelling on the form that his command of the written word was perhaps not the strongest. He may therefore have misunderstood what was being asked and completed the form as best he could – albeit erroneously.

Whatever the relationship between the three, the arrangement did not last much longer and it appears that events had already taken a significant turn, even before James completed the survey. This became apparent when a marriage record from October 1910 was discovered. It clearly shows that Joe Snr quietly remarried in Birmingham – not even a year after Matilda's death. The lady in question was a woman younger than him by around twelve years and who lived not too far away. She was Miss Maud Elizabeth Sidwell.

As far as Maud is concerned, there is no disputing the fact that Joe Snr did subsequently marry again and to a woman of that name. Indeed, Maud became a much-loved grandmother to my mother, who remembers her with great fondness. She eventually passed away in 1954 and survived Joe Snr by about twenty-one years. She lived locally too. In the years just prior to the Great War, her family lived in Cromwell Street – just around a mile or so away from Steam Yard.

However, Joe and Maud's marriage, so soon after Matilda's death, would have been a source of some disquiet. Joe's remarrying so soon after the death of his first wife would have been viewed unfavourably by many in those days. In terms of the family, especially the Hazlewoods, it was very likely to have been taken as an outright act of disrespect in relation to Matilda's memory. By the conventions of the day, they would simply have seen it as too soon.

Consequently, while the 1911 Census shows Joe Snr still living at the Steam Yard address, it also shows a 22-year-old Maud Waite living at 17, Stepney Road – about halfway between Steam Yard and the Sidwell family home in Cromwell Street. The record shows that she declares herself unmarried and to be the sister-in-law of the head of the household, Walter Hill. Also resident is his wife, Eliza. Census information also reveals that, by then, her parents had divorced. Her mother, Mary Ann Sidwell, although still living in Cromwell Street was by then running the local pub, The Bricklayers Arms. Maud Sidwell is no longer listed as resident with her.

Considering the consequences of Joe Snr openly marrying Maud so soon after Matilda's death, it makes sense that the couple quietly married in Birmingham. This was well away from anybody who could have recognised them and who could potentially pass that news on to Joe's family. Furthermore, living apart, but within half a mile of each other, would have at least allowed them to carry on some sort of clandestine relationship, while they avoided public disapproval and worked through the tricky issue of how to tell their families – especially the children.

Of course, the truth came out eventually. Although, it is impossible to say when that might have been and when exactly Joe Snr and Maud finally took on the task of looking after his children. Though, they did eventually become a family and it seems likely that this would have happened sometime before young Joe enlisted. After all, even with the best will in the world, sheer practicality would dictate that keeping a marriage secret for something in the order of four years would have proven tricky to say the least. Nevertheless, something occurred in March 1912 that strongly indicates that the truth about the marriage had still not been shared.

It was reported in the courts columns of both the Coventry Herald and the Midland Daily Telegraph that both Joe Snr and young Joe had appeared at Coventry Magistrates Court, both having been charged with unlawfully and wilfully using a false birth certificate as true. The report in the Midland Daily

Dilapidated buildings in Cow Lane, Coventry, taken around 1936. (*Author's collection*)

Telegraph for 5 March 1912 is the most detailed and in itself, illustrates that both of the Joes were struggling at the time. Whether or not the case reveals the actions of a naïve boy attempting to help his father. Or whether it reveals a father willing to manipulate his son in order to gain extra income is ultimately something for the reader to conclude.

At the time this happened, Joe Snr was living at 18, Cow Lane, in the centre of Coventry. Young Joe, it was reported, was 'living anywhere', until such time as his father had gotten a house. As to the offence, it was explained to the court that the boy Waite had obtained a copy of his birth certificate and that the said certificate had been altered so that the year of birth had been changed to read 1897, instead of 1898. The boy Waite had then used the altered certificate to claim he was 14, the minimum age for factory work, in an attempt to secure work at Middlemore and Lamplugh Ltd, a firm that produced bicycle saddles, horse saddlery and harnesses.

The court was told that Joe Waite had asked his son to obtain the certificate and gave him the money to do so. However, he claimed he had no knowledge of what his son had done with the certificate and gave the boy a good thrashing when he found out what he had done. He therefore pleaded not guilty to the offence. Young Joe had supported his father's plea by saying that he was the guilty party as his father was in 'a lot of trouble' and he therefore wanted to earn some money to help him out. The offence was discovered when, on 2 February 1912, young Joe produced the altered certificate at the factory and the alteration was then noted by Dr Lynes, the physician attending to examine his fitness to work.

When challenged by the doctor, young Joe denied any knowledge of the alteration and maintained that he was fourteen. However, the certificate was subsequently shown to Mr A.P. Oswin, Superintendent for the Foleshill registration district. It was Mr Oswin who confirmed that he had issued the original certificate, which stated the boy's year of birth was 1898 and that the copy had therefore been altered. On that basis, the Registrar General instructed that proceedings should be brought against both Joe and his son.

The outcome of the trial was that Joe Snr was acquitted, with the bench remarking that there had not 'been the slightest bit of evidence offered against him'. Joe therefore thanked the court for what they had done and explained that young Joe's mother had died and lately his son had been staying with friends, but promised not to do such a thing again. When the clerk of the court remarked that the boy should be in school, Joe Snr said that he had sent him to school, but that he had come back to undergo an operation. Young Joe addressed the court and said he was very sorry and was subsequently found guilty and bound over in the sum of £5.00 for six months.

Whatever the truth was behind the case, it is not difficult to see that there were some problems in evidence with the relationship between the two Joes. Furthermore, the question must be asked that, if Joe Snr had no idea what was going on, why, as he freely admitted in court, did he pay for his son to obtain a duplicate birth certificate?

* * *

As a reason to enlist and go off to fight a war, a family row over a pair of boots is probably not one of the most commonly cited motivations you will come across. Nevertheless, as far as young Joe Waite was concerned, that was where it all started. Though, as has now been explained, there were a number of other things going on in the background. Essentially though, that's the account that was always shared within my family: about how a headstrong 16-year-old lad decided that he was going to lie about his age and do his bit for king and country.

It was the autumn of 1914. Young Joe was in the kitchen at home and had set about polishing his boots on the table. That was when his father, Joe Snr, walked in on him. Upon seeing this, his dad certainly had plenty to say to the lad and an almighty row erupted as to just what Joe thought he was up to. You see, even though the family were working class, they, just like their neighbours, had strict standards. As such, polishing boots on kitchen tables would have been viewed as both an extremely unhygienic thing to do and also an open act of disrespect.

Conditions were hard for the working classes of Coventry, but they were nevertheless proud and hard-working people. Many of those who worked in industry were employed in the factories and workshops of what was then a manufacturing powerhouse of a city. Companies such as Daimler, Rudge, Standard and Singer had large factories in the city along with Armstrong-Whitworth, Coventry Chain Co, White and Poppe and Coventry Ordnance Works, all of which by 1914 were gearing up for war production.

These were engineering and manufacturing giants, which turned out everything from trucks, bicycles, bullets, shells, aircraft, bombs and artillery pieces, right up to the 5.5-inch naval guns and massive 15-inch main guns that were used to arm the Royal Navy's most powerful battleships. Indeed, it was exactly this type of engineering work that my family had, by this point, already been engaged in for at least three generations.

At the time of the row, Joe Snr is believed to have been a motor engineer at Daimler's vast plant in the Radford area of the city. It is also highly likely that

The Howitzer Shop at the Royal Ordnance Factory, Red Lane, Coventry. Taken around 1918. (*Author's collection*)

Housewives continuing the practice of scrubbing their doorsteps, possibly from the late 1930s. (*Author's collection*)

young Joe had already been working in the factories from the time he was old enough to do so. However, after all that had gone on, with the death of his mother, his father's clandestine marriage to Maud and whatever difficulties led to their court appearance, I doubt very much that young Joe was particularly happy with his lot. Consequently, it wouldn't have taken much for him to seize any opportunity to try almost anything to get out of the situation he found himself in. It seems then, that what at first comes across as a huge overreaction on his part, was actually more likely to have been the 'straw which broke the camel's back'.

As previously mentioned, though poor, pretty much everybody strove to keep a clean and tidy house. As such, common standards of behaviour and decency were usually proudly observed, with anybody not doing so facing family disapproval. And, dependant on the gravity of the transgression, likely becoming the focus of some very sharp neighbourhood gossip too. After all, this was a time when a housewife's reputation could end up in tatters, simply because a front door step had not been regularly scrubbed and painted.

That said, any close examination of the courts section of the local papers of the day will show that the city's lower classes were no saints either. Drunkenness was clearly a problem, as too was street violence, domestic abuse, and all manner of theft. Nevertheless, while Coventry's lower working class didn't have much and some could be fractious and lawless, many strongly believed that dignity and pride in oneself were things that cost nothing. As such, the idea of polishing a pair of boots in an area where food was prepared was an outrageous affront to their standards. The very idea that it might be acceptable to clean boots there, which had been walking streets covered in industrial grime and animal waste, would have been viewed very dimly indeed. Still, this is what Joe chose to do and it shouldn't therefore be too much of a stretch of the imagination to anticipate what the scale of the reaction from his father might be.

Speculation aside, it is difficult to say for certain why young Joe reacted so strongly, deciding there and then that a row over polishing boots was the right time for him to enlist. Certainly, the fact that he would have also been driven by a strong sense of patriotism and the need to go out and do his bit should not be overlooked. After all, the young men of the city had been enlisting in droves since the outbreak of war in the previous July. Joe had watched all of this and, whether he was 16 or not, it wouldn't have made much difference to him. Just as it hadn't to any number of lads, underage or not, who had already gone before him.

However, I also believe that, by this time, young Joe felt very much embittered by the fact that he was living under the same roof as a woman he resented for replacing his dead mother. Never mind the fact that it had been done in such an underhand way. To make matters worse, he must also have been deeply at odds with a father who had seemingly disrespected Matilda's memory so blatantly by marrying so quickly again. Here then, more than any other reason, would have likely been why young Joe had so wanted to get out from under his father's roof as soon as possible. Finally, as if to underpin the suggestion that a long-standing resentment existed between Maud and at least some of the children, her probate record reveals that the only beneficiary of her estate turned out to be my grandad, George.

If what I have surmised is correct, it isn't so hard to see that whatever patriotic ideals had also driven Joe to take the step towards enlistment, it was a decision that had probably also been motivated by grief, anger and frustration. I therefore think my great-uncle's first steps to war were also taken with a heavy heart.

Chapter 2

The British Army of 1914

By the time Joe Waite signed up in November 1914 and took the King's Shilling, his battalion, the 1/7th Bn (TF) the Royal Warwickshire Regiment, was already well engaged in preparations to join the fighting in France. The unit itself was based at Coventry's Queen Victoria Road Drill Hall and recruited pretty much exclusively from the city and its surrounding areas. However, it is worth noting at this point that the unit was not a 'Pals Battalion', as has sometimes been suggested. This is because, although recruited from a specific catchment, they were not one that came into being as a result of a number of wartime national recruitment initiatives. Instead, at the onset of war, the 1/7th Royal Warwicks were already an established unit. Therefore, before we look at Joe's service more closely, it is worth examining the distinctions between the various elements that made up the army's fighting strength.

In 1914, as with those men who were already a part of a unit, all men who enlisted into Territorial Force (TF) units gave an undertaking to complete a minimum training and attendance commitment for each year, including a two-week annual camp. At the outbreak of the war, the 1/7th Royal Warwicks was actually away on annual camp, in the area of Rhyl in North Wales. It was

Queen Victoria Road Drill Hall, seen here around the 1960s. (*Author's collection*)

immediately called back to Coventry where it quickly completed preparations for war mobilisation, before leaving the city again around the middle of August 1914.

From there, it found itself stationed in the town of Witham, close to Chelmsford in Essex. It was here that the unit commenced the training that would bring the existing men up to combat readiness and continue to receive and train a steady flow of newly enlisted recruits. Joining them in the Chelmsford area were three other TF units: the 1/5, 1/6 & 1/8 battalions of the Royal Warwicks. Together they formed the Warwickshire Brigade of the South Midland Division. Although, on 13 May 2015, soon after arriving in France, the battalions collectively became the 143rd Brigade of the 48th (South Midland) Division.

What made TF units distinct from regular or reserve units were the subsequent prefixes added to their battalion number. For instance, in this case, the first line unit of the 7th battalion Royal Warwicks became the 1/7. This followed the creation of a second line unit, the 2/7 battalion and later a 3/, or reserve element, was also created. However, it is exclusively the service of the 1/7 Royal Warwicks that will be followed in this work, given that the 2/7 has its own distinct combat history, initially as part of the 2nd Warwickshire Brigade of the 2nd (South Midland) Division.

As to the TF itself, (known from 1921 as the Territorial Army, or TA), this had been specifically formed in 1908 as part of the Haldane Reforms. Named after the then Secretary of State for War, Richard Burdon Haldane, these changes were implemented from 1906 onwards. The intention was to improve the effectiveness of the British Army, particularly with regard to overseas deployment during times of war. As it transpired, it would be only eight years before the war clouds gathered and Haldane's vision would be put to the ultimate test.

At the outbreak of the Great War, Britain's Army Reserve numbered around 210,000 men. That is to say, men who had previously served with the Colours but who still retained a reserve liability and, as such, could

Richard Burdon Haldane, whose military reforms led to the creation of the Territorial Force. (*Public domain*)

be recalled to the Colours. Added to this was the regular British Army, which was a comparatively small force of professional soldiers, numbering around 247,500 men worldwide.

A sizeable contingent of that regular strength, comprising six Infantry Divisions with Cavalry and ancillary support units and numbering around 100,000 – 120,000 men, was sent to France at the outbreak of the war. This number does not include the subsequent additions to fighting strength provided by forces from across the British Empire, such as those from India, Australia, New Zealand, Canada, Africa and so many other Imperial dominions that sent their men to fight in the service of the king.

That original force, the British Expeditionary Force or BEF as it was known, was subsequently pretty much wiped out in the early months of the war. Indeed, by the end of 1914, it had suffered catastrophic losses of around 90,000 men. Therefore, the ability to quickly replace those losses with reservists and also deploy additional units to the front was vital. Consequently, the use of the TF seemed an obvious choice. Though, that option came with certain complications.

At its formation, the TF was only ever intended exclusively as a home defence force, freeing the regular army and reserves from responsibility for that role and allowing them instead to concentrate fully on overseas operations. As such, the complication that arose with the TF at the outbreak of hostilities was two-fold. First, since the formation of the units themselves, there had been recruitment problems, which resulted in many of the units being well under strength by the time war broke out. Second, all of the men were volunteers and the terms of service under which they signed up allowed them the option of declining to serve overseas. As such, units that were already well under strength were even further depleted in terms of deployable numbers when significant numbers opted not to volunteer for overseas service.

Chief among their reasons not to go, particularly where more skilled men were concerned, was the issue of pay. It is not too difficult to understand why a skilled man with a family to support would not want to forfeit his civilian wage. This is because it was typically likely to be far better than the relatively poor pay that the army provided to its regular soldiers. Furthermore, the loss would be increased by the fact that the civilian wage was also being supplemented by the additional income paid by the TF.

With such a significant drop in income, the decision to volunteer for overseas service would mean that the subsequent reduction in money coming into the house might bring genuine hardship upon the men's families. As such, it would make that choice completely untenable. However, the choice not to serve overseas did not mean that these men could not serve in some other capacity. Many would instead remain behind at their unit bases, staying on to serve as part of a further reserve contingent and fulfilling the original role of the TF as a home defence force.

While the issues connected to the overseas deployment of volunteers who had already enlisted prior to the war could prove problematic, those men enlisting after the outbreak of war came with no such complications. Particularly as the majority of them knew full well they were signing up to fight overseas. This is best evidenced by documents found in the surviving service records of soldiers signing up to serve with the 1/7 Royal Warwicks, towards the end of 1914.

The records confirm that any man volunteering to serve with the battalion initially signed a standard TF Attestation form. This recorded the man's basic details, place of enlistment and the date. It was also signed by both the recruit and the attesting officer. Normally, this in itself committed the recruit to four years' service within the United Kingdom, thereby preventing him from being posted overseas. However, upon signing the attestation form, the recruit would also sign Army Form E624 at the same time.

Essentially, this acted as a waiver as it provided the means whereby the recruit forfeited his option to remain within the UK and instead accepted liability for an overseas posting. The particulars of the form were worded thus:

AGREEMENT to be made by an officer or man of the Territorial Force to subject himself to liability to serve in any place outside the United Kingdom in the event of national emergency.

This was then followed by the actual legal declaration itself:

I... (Full particulars of soldier and unit) – do hereby agree, subject to the conditions stated overleaf, to accept liability, in the event of national emergency, to serve in any place outside the United Kingdom, in accordance with the provisions of Section XIII. (2) (a) of the Territorial and Reserve Forces Act, 1907.

The form was then signed by both the soldier and his commanding officer and the date and location of the signature recorded at the foot of the form.

Essentially, the liability set out on the rear of the form confirmed that the soldier would agree to serve, wherever he was required to do so, for the duration of his service. Though the tenure of service would eventually be amended as being for the 'duration of the war'. Interestingly, it also specified that the soldier, although agreeing to serve anywhere, could only be expected to do so with either the unit in which he enlisted, or a part of that unit. Though the necessities of war would eventually change this, he could not at this time be compelled to serve in any other unit under the terms of that agreement. In addition any soldier signing the form, was to be awarded a badge that was to be worn on the right breast of his uniform,

Territorial Force Imperial Service badge. (*Author's collection*)

clearly showing that he had agreed to serve overseas. However, the wearing of the Territorial Force Imperial Service Badge, as it became known, was not compulsory.

From the point of view of the battalion, the efforts to recruit more men had proven very successful indeed. Nominally, by the time the 1/7 was ready to take ship to France, it had a full complement of 30 officers and 1,003 other ranks.

With conscription not being introduced until January 1916, other ways had to be found early on in the war to swell the ranks of the army. This was done very successfully with an ongoing cycle of both national and local recruiting campaigns. The most notable of these was the campaign headed by the then Secretary of State for War, Lord Herbert Kitchener. His famous 'Your Country Needs You' poster campaign prompted tens of thousands of men to enlist after war started and saw the formation of an entirely separate volunteer army. This 'new army', sometimes referred to as 'Kitchener's Mob', was an entirely separate entity to both the regular army, the reserve and the TF. Albeit, its newly formed units did take their identities from existing British Army regiments and were often referred to as 'Service Battalions'.

A further, if ill-fated element of British combat strength, the Pals Battalions, were also created around the

A variant of the famous recruitment poster, featuring Lord Kitchener. (*Public domain*)

start of the war. These were men who were recruited from very specific parts of the populace; such as small towns, factories, sporting groups, institutions, trades or occupations. All under the premise that men who associated in civilian life would bond and fight better as a military unit than strangers might.

Over a tenth of the British battalions raised in the Great War were 'Pals' battalions. Units like the Grimsby Chums, the Sheffield City Battalion, the Accrington Pals and even an element of the Royal Warwicks, the Birmingham Pals, all ended up on the Western Front. Though, as soon as fighting started in earnest, the tragic flaw behind the concept of the Pals battalions would become grimly apparent, particularly during the Somme offensive.

As an example, the Accrington Pals, with a fighting strength of 700 men, were ordered to attack Serre on the first day of the battle – 1 July 1916. Within the first twenty minutes of that action, 235 were killed, with a further 350 wounded. Furthermore, the battalion had gone into action with other units from Sheffield, Leeds, Barnsley and Bradford, all of whom also suffered heavy casualties. The net result was that whole communities were left devasted by the loss of so many men from their midst. Some had literally lost a whole generation of men. Consequently, it was soon realised that, though well-intentioned, the thinking behind the formation of the Pals was badly flawed and recruiting for these units was permanently ended.

It is worthy of note at this stage to recognise that, although they were later lowered, standards of medical fitness were rigorously applied within the enlistment process for the various units. Conversely, the checks to establish whether a potential recruit was of the correct age were clearly not as thorough. Ultimately, even though the minimum age for overseas service was 19 years of age, around 250,000 underage volunteers would eventually go on to serve in the British armed forces.

A final detail that separated the various elements of the army was the issue of service numbers. As with the Regular Army, the TF issued numbers up to four figures long. Though not an issue with the men of Kitchener's armies or the Pals, who were normally issued five-figure numbers, it did cause issues, particularly with the administration of TF battalions. This was because separate units generally used service numbers that would be repeated in other units. Confusion could then arise if, for instance, Private 1234 Smith was transferred to a different regiment, where a soldier already had the service number 1234. Though not entirely eliminating the risk of repetition, this was greatly reduced in early 1917, when all TF units were renumbered with six-figure service numbers, allocated in blocks to separate units. As will become clearer later, this proved to be a more efficient system.

Chapter 3

Marching to War

Though the exact date as to when Joe Waite enlisted is not known, the subsequent reappearance of his name in the Coventry Herald helped significantly in narrowing this down. When he joined up, Joe was issued with the service number 3165. This number already indicated enlistment around November 1914, when compared to men with similar service numbers whose enlistment dates are known.

However, the Coventry Herald article of 6 & 7 November 1914 places it more accurately as early November, or possibly even late October. The article, headed 'Better Recruiting', with the subtitle of 'More Men for Regulars and Territorials', reports on the success of the most recent recruitment drives in the city. More particularly, it hails the success of recruitment to the 7th (Reserve) battalion of the Royal Warwickshire Regiment and states that only a further 228 men were needed to bring the unit to full strength. The article highlights the fact that no less than 44 men joined the battalion on Monday (2 November) and goes on to provide a list of 209 men, recruited since 20 October. Included in the list is the name Joseph James Waite.

On the day of his enlistment, it is likely that Joe was given a medical, which clearly did not pick up on the fact he was underage. He would probably also have been attested (sworn in) and embodied the same day. This would mean that, from that point, he was classed as being part of the battalion strength. As such, it would not be very long before he was on a train, along with his fellow recruits, and en route to the battalion training camp at Witham, Essex.

Once at Witham, Joe would have found himself subjected to standard infantry soldier training. This was a revolving programme of such things as drill, fieldcraft, musketry, route marches, fitness training and trench construction. For some recruits, the mastery of basic soldiering would then be followed by more specialised training, based on the needs of the battalion at the time. Though the list of specialisms is long, it would include such things as animal handling, the operation of Lewis and Vickers Machine Guns, and signalling. Men would also have been assessed for their potential for promotion to non-commissioned officer (NCO) ranks.

A contingent of the 7th Bn Royal Warwicks prepare to depart from Coventry railway station. The type of rifles carried indicate that this is likely to be between 1914-15. (*Public domain*)

Soldiers of the Royal Warwicks on Radford Range, Coventry. The site later became the Daimler airfield. The rifles used are either Lee Metford or Mk1 Lee Enfield (Long Lee), which are, visually, almost identical. (*Public domain*)

Launched in 1907 and owned by the Great Eastern Railway Co, the steamer SS *Copenhagen* was used as both a troop ship and hospital ship. Along with her companion ship, the SS *City of Lucknow*, she ferried the 1/7 Royal Warwicks to Le Havre. Both ships were subsequently sunk by enemy action later in the war. SS *City of Lucknow* was torpedoed and sunk on 21 December 1917, sixty miles east of Malta by U21. Fortunately, her entire crew of 42 were subsequently rescued by the destroyer, HMS *Rifleman*. The crew of the SS *Copenhagen* were less fortunate. She was torpedoed earlier that year by U61 in the North Sea on 5 March 1917, eight miles east of the Noord Hinder Lightship, and sank with the loss of six lives. (*Public domain*)

By the time March 1915 had come around, the battalion was able to ship a full complement of fully trained men to France. And so, on 22 March, 30 officers and 1,003 ordinary ranks (ORs) left Witham, bound for Southampton. Most of those men boarded the SS *Copenhagen*, with a further 52 men and one officer boarding the SS *City of Lucknow*. Then, at 0530 hours that evening, the ships steamed out of the Solent and sailed for the French port of Le Havre.

After a night crossing of the English Channel the men safely disembarked and eventually moved out to Armentieres for training. However, for Joe Waite, crossing with the battalion that day was not an option. He was still undergoing training and it was not until 25 June that he landed in France as part of a reinforcement party of a further 100 men. From there, he joined his battalion in early July, where they were engaged in training at Lozinghem, in the Pas De Calais region of France.

By the time of Joe's arrival, the 1/7 Royal Warwicks had already lost 19 men to enemy action. Their first loss had been Private 2275, Jesse Duckett, from Coventry. He was killed on 29 April after the enemy shelled the positions the unit was occupying at Steenbeck trenches, close to Wulverghem. The following month the battalion lost a further ten men, again during the shelling of Steenbeck trenches. It was here that Private 2406 John Adams, the youngest known battalion casualty of the entire war, was killed on 9 May. John was from Fazely in Staffordshire and he was just 16 years old. The following month, a further eight men were killed while serving at either Wulverghem or Ploegsteert.

Because Joe's service record no longer exists, there is mostly no way of knowing the exact details of where he served. Certainly, the battalion war diary is the only means of surmising what he may have been involved in. However, though the diary is a clear chronology of events, it is not possible to say that Joe was present at any particular time. This is because there is no way to account

Lance Corporal Joe Waite (centre rear) seen with his comrades and Lewis Gun. The actual date and location of the photo is unknown. (*Waite family archive*)

for any time Joe spent away from the unit for such things as leave, specialist training, or illness and injury. Any reference to the war diary is therefore on the assumption that Joe was likely present. There are, though, some exceptions to that rule, given that there is photographic evidence that Joe probably trained to be part of a Lewis Gun team at some stage. Also, Joe himself had confirmed in conversations with family that he fought during both the Somme campaign and at the Battle of Passchendaele.

With that in mind, it is likely that Joe's first experience of life in a front-line trench began on 25 July 1915, when the battalion took over trenches at Hebuterne. However, it is possible that either by then or soon after, Joe would have received some bad news from home. His only surviving grandfather, Joseph Waite, had been admitted to the Coventry Union Workhouse on 29 April and being classed as 'infirm' was likely sent to the workhouse infirmary. On 20 July, after three days of being of 'unsound mind', he too died in the workhouse, just as Joe's other grandfather, Samuel Hazlewood, had in 1906.

From their very first day in the Hebuterne Sector trenches, Joe and his comrades had to endure miserable conditions. Not only was the weather bad, with continual thunderstorms, but the trenches themselves were in a poor state and lacked much of the basic kit and facilities to make them habitable. However, despite a two-day extension to the relief, things went without any serious problems and they were relieved on 31 July by the 1/7 Worcesters.

What followed from there was typical of life for front-line infantry units. That was a regular round of relieving and holding trenches, interspersed with periods of limited rest, training and frequent work parties. Exposure to enemy fire was just that – artillery and small arms fire, as opposed to any sort of concerted attack on positions, mounted either by British or German forces. Indeed, although men were wounded, there would not be any further men lost until two men were killed during September and a further six were killed in October. All of these men were either killed by snipers, or by shelling and trench mortar fire. With just a further two men being killed in December, the battalion was relieved from trenches at Foncquevillers on 19 December. From there, the men spent their first Christmas at the front as brigade reserve, before going back into the trenches, the day after Boxing Day.

The first half of 1916 did not really differ from what the battalion had experienced since landing in France. Both sides continued to bring fire down on each other in the usual manner and the unit functioned as normal, rotating its duties between the front line and rear positions. Occasional skirmishes were recorded, but these were generally as a result of patrolling by both sides and trench raiding. Though, casualties were so low in general that individual names were still being recorded in the battalion war diary and those who fell were still being recovered for burial. Indeed, between New Year and 1 July, the battalion suffered the loss of only 21 men killed.

The one occurrence within that period that would make a real difference to the battalion was on 13 May 1916. The war diary simply recalls: 'Wet day. Bathing. Issue of short rifles.' The short rifle referred to was in fact the .303 Mk III Short Magazine Lee Enfield (SMLE).

This very matter-of-fact entry belies the great importance of what happened that day. Prior to the issue of the 'short rifles', many TF units had been using the Mk 1 Lee Enfield, or 'Long Lee'. Although mechanically similar to its successor, the rifle was not well thought of and where soldiers could, they would discard the Long Lee if they came across the Mk III SMLE. As far as the new rifle was concerned, it was a game-changer. The Mk III SMLE and its later variants are still regarded as probably the finest bolt-action combat rifles ever designed. Their ability to transform the firepower and marksmanship of the individual soldier vastly increased the combat effectiveness of units, as they were issued with the new rifles.

Unlike the standard German rifle, the Mauser Gewehr 1898, which held only five rounds and had a more cumbersome action, the Mk III SMLE had a ten-round magazine and a very fluid bolt action which allowed the soldier to maintain his sight picture while operating the bolt to eject and load another round. The result was that the British infantryman became capable of performing the 'mad minute'. This meant that, in the space of just one minute, a soldier could get off between twenty and thirty aimed shots. On occasions where 'rapid fire' was ordered, this capability caused many enemy units, so far unused to coming up against Mk III SMLE-equipped troops, to believe that they were actually coming under machine-gun fire.

As mentioned, either side of the issue of the new rifle, life for the 1/7 Royal Warwicks changed little in the run-up to July 1916. Essentially, they remained in the wider Somme sector, moving around positions close to towns and villages like Gezaincourt, Couin, Souastre, Hebuterne and Courcelle. Yet, for

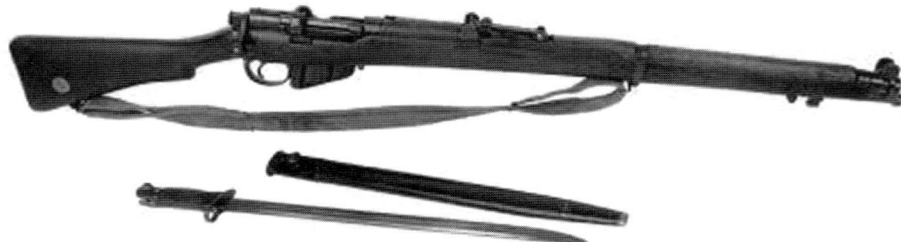

The Mk. III Short Magazine Lee Enfield (SMLE) with 1907 pattern British bayonet. (*Author's collection*)

Although likely a posed photo, this shows a Lewis Gun team from the 48th South Midland Division. The Somme, 1916. (*Public domain*)

them, as with all of the other units on the Western Front, the nature of the war was about to change dramatically.

On 22 June, having spent ten days at Couin engaged in training and working parties, the battalion moved back into its previously occupied positions at G Sector trenches, Hebuterne. Two days later, at 0500 hours, British artillery, all along the front, commenced a week-long bombardment of German positions, heralding the build-up to the first day of the Battle of the Somme.

Anyone with any knowledge of the Great War will know that, on 1 July 1916, the British army suffered the worst day in its history. After the artillery had ceased its shelling and several huge mines had been detonated under enemy positions, British and Imperial forces went over the top and advanced into the teeth of a ferocious German defence, which had hardly been dented by the millions of shells landing on it over the past week. The result was carnage, with British casualties numbering 57,470 on the first day, of which 19,240 were killed. However, the 1/7 Royal Warwicks lost just six men that day, as they had been tasked with holding their positions and not therefore tasked with attacking any German positions.

There is of course no way to understand how the men felt, both from the point of view of watching the ill-fated assault unfold and in enduring the German counterfire on their positions. However, the war diary entry for the day does give some idea of its truly awful nature.

Fine day. Attack on 4th Army front commenced 7.00am. This battn's role is to hold G Sector trenches. The left of the 4th army attack being in our immediate right. We let off smoke and phosphorous bombs to mask fire of enemy opposite us. Our troops met with success at first – many conflicting reports came through during day. The trenches were shelled heavily from about 7.35 am through to about 9.30am but after that were only subjected to very intermittent shelling. Many phosphorous bombs set alight by a shell. No casualties among the bomb throwers. We provided a party of 65 O.R. and officer to carry up ammunition for 4" Stokes guns which were to move forward when flank consolidates, but no consolidation took place. They did not leave our trenches. There were 19 casualties (of whom 4 killed) in this party. In the two Coys holding in trenches there were only 3 casualties during the day. The enemy dropped 2 tear gas shells in proximity of Battn HQ but did no harm to those near. "NO MANS LAND" on our right strewn with bodies after the attack. Many wounded and try to crawl back & are sniped at by Germans opposite us. (Reported by Lt E.W. FOWLER). Many stragglers and wounded return to our right Coy trenches.during morning more dealt with by B & C Coy. Draft of 14 officers joins battn – remain at transport lines for the night & come to HEBUTERNE for the 2nd. All of them 3rd DORSETS except one of 1/1 HUNTS CYCLISTS.

Obviously, the role of a war diary is to report facts and not to record thoughts or feelings as to the events. That aside, it is easy enough to see from the entry that the day was like nothing the men had ever seen before. However, though they had witnessed such carnage, it would be mere days before they themselves would experience what it was like to charge upon heavily defended German positions. That time would come on 14 July, which was the opening day of the Battle of Bazentin Ridge – one of the many smaller battles fought up to the conclusion of the Somme campaign on 18 November 1916. It would be the worst day of the war for the battalion so far.

On the previous day, they had moved by lorry to a position outside Bouzincourt and from there to the village of Albert. At midnight, the battalion lay down in a field and waited for 0730 hours, the time they would move up to the village of La Boiselle and launch an attack on the enemy. By the time the attack was launched, on time, the battalion had already been heavily shelled and had suffered casualties. The war diary describes the assault as follows:

Moved into position in trenches and were heavily shelled going into LA BOISELLE. At 7.30am after artillery preparation A & B Coys proceeded to assault. They reached their objective. Many casualties resulted, chiefly from machine guns, the following officer being killed. 2/Lt BULLOCK and the following attached officers of the 3rd DORSET Regt. Lt JONES, 2nd Lt BAKER, 2nd Lt FORMAN. We held the trench for seven hours when we had to evacuate it on account of the enemy's extremely heavy enfilade fire both shell and machine guns. Lieut Col KNOX who led the attack and who had shown the greatest bravery throughout was wounded later. Maj HANSON then took command of the battn. Our casualties estimated at 150 of whom 68 were reported killed.

Essentially, the attack marked a turning point for the battalion. Not only was it the deadliest day they had experienced so far, but the sheer number of casualties meant that the recording of individual names was no longer possible. Furthermore, the opportunity to recover bodies from the battlefield and give them a proper burial was also no longer possible and the practice of leaving many of the men where they fell became a matter of simple necessity.

By the end of the month of July, CWGC records reveal that the battalion lost 91 men, including one attack on German trenches on 25 & 26 July when 22 men were killed. Overall, by the end of the Somme campaign, a total of 133 men, which is a little more than a tenth of its full strength, had been killed. Furthermore, with the men in poor condition and trench foot prevalent throughout the unit, they were just about to enter a freezing cold winter – the coldest in France since 1892.

For the battalion, much of the mid-winter months of December 1916 and January 1917 were spent in training. It was not until 1 February that they returned to the front line, relieving the French army in trenches at Eclusier. From there, interspersed with just a few days' break, they spent the remainder of the month on the front line. Moving into spring and early summer, life for the men of the unit was then the usual rotation of rest, working parties and front-line duty.

On 22 June 1917, having lost a further thirty-seven men over the last months, the battalion was pulled from its trenches on the Morchies-Baumetz Line and was initially held in reserve at Beugny. By the thirtieth, they were marching towards Bedford Camp at Gomiecourt. There they engaged in nearly three weeks of training before marching to Halloy and then on to Authieule, where they entrained for the military rail hub at Proven in Belgium. Apart from a brief period of training in September 1917 and a brief redeployment to the Vimy Ridge sector in late October, the battalion would not return to France for the duration of the war.

After arriving at Proven, the battalion marched to nearby Sint-Jan-ter-Biezen, a small village just outside of Poperinghe, where they would complete their latest period of training. By month's end, they had taken their first steps onto the battlefields of the Ypres Salient, just as the Third Battle of Ypres, or Passchendaele as it is often called, had begun.

Having been in the field since the start of August 1917, the battalion did not suffer any losses until the tenth, when they relieved the 1/5 Royal Warwicks in trenches on the St Julien Sector. With one man killed that day, the battalion lost a further eight men the following day when they were heavily shelled by both high explosive and mustard gas shells. Losses steadily mounted as the month progressed, until the worst day when, on 27 August, C and D Company (Coy) attacked an objective known as Springfield Farm. Although successful, the attack cost those companies a total of thirty men killed. Eventually, by the end of August, the Battle of Passchendaele had already cost the unit a further eighty men killed.

With a month of experience on the battlefields of Belgium, the unit was withdrawn from the field and back into France for a further month's training. Billeted at La Panne, the men were put through their paces in various battalion attack exercises until, at the end of the month, they were returned to Belgium, finally taking up position in shelters on the western side of the Yser Canal, just on the outskirts of the city of Ypres. There, they waited for the order to advance once more.

Chapter 4

The Battle of Broodseinde

Though never intended to be a definitive battalion history, it is perhaps important to add some further historical detail at this point in order to create context, particularly as to the various component parts of the British and Imperial forces operating in the Ypres salient during 1917.

The Third Battle of Ypres began on 31 July 1917 and lasted for over three months before finally ending on 10 November 1917. The campaign was chiefly prosecuted by the British Fifth Army under the command of General Hubert Gough. As well as fielding British troops, the army also included troops from New Zealand, Australia and Canada, serving across fifty divisions. There was also a French element numbering some six divisions.

Part of XVIII Corps, one of those divisions was the 48th (South Midland) Division, which was made up of three separate TF infantry brigades. These were the 143rd (Warwickshire) Brigade, the 144th (Gloucester and Worcester) Brigade and the 145th (South Midland) Brigade. It was the 143rd to which the 1/7 Royal Warwicks belonged, along with the 1/5, 1/6 and 1/8 battalions of the Royal Warwicks. Additional units within the division were the 143rd Machine Gun Coy and the 143rd Trench Mortar Battery.

The campaign was conducted across several smaller battles within the larger context of the overall battle strategy. In simple terms, the intention was to gradually take and hold ground from the German army, which, in large part, proved successful. However, the offensive itself was a controversial plan from the outset, with opposition from British Prime Minister David Lloyd George and various allied chiefs-of-staff as to the choice of army used, the location and the

General Sir Hubert Gough, GCB, GCMG, KCVO. (*Public domain*)

timings. Such is the controversial nature of what happened at that time, that the battle is still hotly debated to this day. However, whilst it remains the preserve of historians and tacticians to perpetually argue the various tactical and historical pros and cons, there is no argument to refute that the battle itself was an utter hell upon earth for all of those involved on the ground.

A combination of bad weather, poor soil conditions and the relentless artillery bombardments that shattered any ability for the ground to drain naturally created a vast, crater-pocked swamp. Here, men often fought from shell holes rather than trenches, and it was a place where tanks, men, guns, and horses struggled to operate. Moreover, the Flanders mud was a killer in its own right. There are many accounts of it sucking men down to an appalling death. Particularly if they were so unfortunate as to stray off firm ground or duck boards, into the vast stretches of thick, deep muck.

By the time the Battle of Broodseinde began on 4 October, conditions on the ground were about as bad as could be. However, buoyed up by previous successes, the British would go ahead with the intention of capturing the Broodseinde ridge and completing the capture of the Gheluvelt plateau. These locations lay to the east of Ypres and formed part of a series of low ridges that

A soldier negotiates his way through the treacherous mud and water-filled shell holes of the shattered Flanders landscape of 1917. (*Public domain*)

overlooked the town. The presence of the Germans in these positions left British forces at a disadvantage, in that the British were occupying the lower ground and were therefore overlooked. Consequently, taking the ridgelines to the east of the town would prove highly advantageous and push the Germans further east, eventually allowing the allies to capture the key objective of the village of Passchendaele.

The battle line itself was vast, running along eight miles, from just above Gheluvelt at its southern end, up to the villages of Poelcapelle and Langemarck at its northern end. Gough's Fifth Army would push forward on the northern extremity. The Second Army, under the command of General Herbert Plumer and including the 1st and 2nd ANZAC Corps, would push from the southern end, up to the British Fifth Army right flank, just below Poelcapelle. This offensive zone covered just around two-thirds of the overall battle line, accounting for why the battle is so important in the fighting history of the ANZAC (Australia New Zealand Army Corps) forces today.

As the time to attack approached, the 1/7 Royal Warwicks made their final preparations. They had already moved into position close to the Yser Canal on 2 October and from there, the battalion moved closer to its jump-off point. They would then press on to take key objectives, including the two enemy strongpoints of Terrier Farm and Tweed House.

Code names existed for many different types of locations, both Allied and German, on the front and could refer to a number of different types of location. As for the named German strongpoints, many of these existed along the front and represented a number of different types of structures. For instance, Terrier Farm was likely to have been a bombed-out farmhouse that had been turned into a machine-gun-equipped, reinforced strongpoint by the Germans. The site still exists today, though no trace of fortification remains and a small farmhouse now stands on the site. Tweed House is more likely to have been what is referred to as a 'Mebus', or concrete-reinforced machine gun post. Though, other structures such as nests and dugouts, sometimes disguised as timber piles, could also be encountered, along with much larger, purpose-built, concrete blockhouses.

It should, however, be noted that none of these structures survive today. There are still a good number of concrete fortifications in the wider area, though the ones on the land below Poelcapelle have long since disappeared. They were likely broken up post-war by local farmers, either for building materials and hardcore, or to clear the land for farming. Nevertheless, their existence in October 1917 would prove to be highly significant in relation to the events that were about to unfold and the battalion war diary recounts in detail what happened next:

British troops pass by the corpse of a soldier outside an abandoned German bunker. The structure shown is likely very similar in design to Tweed House. (*Public domain*)

3 October 1917 – North East Of Ypres.

Battle stores were drawn and issued during the morning. At 6pm head of Battalion passed BRIDGE 2a and moved up to MON DU HIBOU via the trench board track past ALBERTA. At HIBOU a guide from 1/1 Bucks Regt met companies and led them to FLORACOT to assembly positions. No difficulty was experienced and in this operation four casualties only were suffered. The night was very suitable a bright moon being overcast by clouds leaving sufficient light to see quite well without making movement visible to the enemy.

The battalion was in position on a taped line of shell holes laid out by Capt BUSHILL 12.30 midnight. The positions were as follows:

D Company in two lines. Two platoons in front and two in rear about [grid ref] V25 C92.

C company two platoons in front and two in rear astride HUBNER-QUEBEC ROAD D1 G16.

A Company 200 yards in rear of D Coy and B Coy 200 yards in rear of C Coy.

Bn Headquarters was established at HUBNER.

4th of October 1917

Remainder of the night was quiet. At 5.30am the enemy put down a heavy barrage on and about the LANGEMARCK LINE.

At 6am our barrage came down and the attack commenced. C & D Coys attacking the first objective, a line from V25 G91 to V26 C41 and including TWEED HOUSE.

C company on the right experienced great difficulty on account of bad ground, numerous shell holes and very wet. At about D2 A71 their right was held up by a machine gun. Here Capt CROALL was killed and the company sustained many casualties. The left pushed on Lt NICHOLLS assuming command of the Company. The left support platoon was put out to form a defensive flank and deal with the M.G. holding up the right. After about half an hours fighting the M.G was captured and the enemy either killed or captured.

The Company then pushed on again capturing 10 prisoners about V26 C93.

It was difficult to locate their position accurately and the Company found they had reached the CEMETERY. Finding they were in our own barrage they withdrew to a line V26 C48 to V26 C72 which they consolidated.

D Company on the left advanced well and without much opposition at first. They were then held up by an M.G. at TWEED HOUSE. Both gun and team were captured. The Company pushed on again to its objective and seized it and consolidated a line from V26 A22 to V26 C38 joining with C Coy on the right and and the 9th LANC FUS on the left. 2 Lt BRANT was wounded in this operation.

The remaining two Companies, A & B, who were to attack the second objective kept as well up to the barrage as possible without becoming involved in the fighting for the first objectives.

B Company on the right pushed forward to a line about V26 G13 along the front edge of the road and far side of the CEMETERY taking a few prisoners.

They found this line could not be held. Both flanks were in the air and the protective barrage had settled on the CEMETERY. They therefore withdrew to a line V26 C98 to V26 D17, linking up with the 6th Bn R WAR R. on the right at V26 C93.

A Company on the left pushed forward close after the barrage captured TERRIER FARM and then advanced to a line from V26 A98 to V26 G11 meeting with strong enemy resistance at V26 G13. A party of men attacked this point and captured one officer and about 50 other ranks. This company also pushed on too far and got into the protective barrage so withdrew to a line V26 A75 through COUNTY CROSS ROADS to V26 C95 linking up with the 9th LANC FUS on the left and B company on the right.

A large enemy party formed up near GLOSTER HOUSE and counter attacked the 9th LANCS FUS. This was met and completely broken up by our own Lewis Gun and rifle fire.

Three small counter attacks started from BEEK HOUSE but they were all dispersed by our fire.

Two other attacks started from V26 A76 were also smashed.

Two Vickers M guns were got into position near TWEED HOUSE where they could sweep the whole of our front.

Advanced Bn Hd Qrs were established at TWEED HOUSE.

As can be seen, the account of the initial attack and the fighting that followed is quite detailed. It confirms that the battalion initially advanced behind a protective barrage before determinedly engaging the enemy to secure its objectives, despite initial heavy losses. The diary does not make any reference to any individuals who were later recommended for bravery awards. However, it is at this point in the attack that Joe Waite is thought to have neutralised one of the machine guns that had wrought so much havoc on the advancing men. Through that action, he would later be awarded the MM.

The citation for Joe's award has not been located. This is not unusual as many MM citations from the Great War have since been lost. Instead, his award was originally listed on page 844 of the Supplement for the London Gazette, dated 14 January 1918. But, one citation from that day does exist and dovetails well with the account given in the battalion war diary. That is the citation for the award of the VC to Joe's comrade and fellow Coventry lad, Private Arthur Hutt. Arthur's VC was one of a total of nine that were awarded over the three days that the Battle of Broodseinde took place. The citation reads as follows:

For most conspicuous bravery and initiative in attack, when all the officers and non-commissioned officers of No. 2 platoon having become casualties, Pte. Hutt took command of and led forward the platoon. He was held up by a strong post on his right, but immediately ran forward alone in front of the platoon and shot the officer and three men in the post, causing between forty and fifty others to surrender. Later, realising that he had pushed too far,

Corporal Arthur Hutt. The first and so far only native of Coventry to be awarded the Victoria Cross. (*Public domain*) *he withdrew his party. He personally covered the withdrawal by sniping the enemy, killing a number and then carried back a badly wounded man and put him under shelter. Pte. Hutt then organised and consolidated his position, and learning that some wounded men were lying out and likely to become prisoners if left there, no stretcher bearers being available, he went out and carried in four wounded men under heavy fire.*

Originally published in the Fourth Supplement to The London Gazette of 23 November 1917. 26 November 1917, Numb. 30400, p. 12330

Eventually, through the brave efforts of the men, the battalion was able to secure its objectives. However, from that point on they would have to wait and hold their positions for a further three days before they were relieved. The war diary describes those days as follows:

5 October 1917
Rain fell during the day and the weather became very cold. No enemy attack took place but his shelling was very severe at times. Sniping was active on both sides. The enemy firing continually from BEEK HOUSE. At night a dry change of socks was got up together with rations.

6 October 1917
Rain still continued which together with the cold made conditions very difficult and trying. Enemy posts were located near OXFORD HOUSE and BEEK HOUSE, between BEEK HOUSE and the CEMETERY and a machine gun post in the CEMETERY. BURNS HOUSE was reported to be strongly held. Very little enemy movement took place.

7 October 1917 – Irish Farm
Rain fell again most of the day. Enemy shelling was heavy, growing into a barrage towards evening. No infantry action followed.

A taped track was marked out from MON DU HIBOU to TWEED HOUSE. At night the Battalion was relieved by 1/1 BUCKS REGT and moved into bivouacs near IRISH FARM. Everyone being in by 4am.

Doubtless, by the time the battalion had been pulled out of the field, the men were pretty much exhausted – both physically and mentally. Initially, they were moved from Irish Farm to a position in the rear called Siege Camp. From there they moved to billets in Poperinghe. Nevertheless, it is known that even after that action, the men were still used in working parties and many casualties are attributed to 8 October, just one day after they were withdrawn.

When a casualty summary was recorded in the war diary on 11 October, the list of men killed, wounded and missing paints a chilling picture of the true cost of the operation.

Company parades and kit inspections. Reorganisation carried on with. Weather cold but fine.
Casualties during operations were:

Killed Capt J.J. CROALL 5th R.S.F.
2 Lt H.R. ROGERS
Other ranks 23
Wounded:
2/LT BENNETT
2/LT BRANT
2/LT HEARN temporarily attached 6Bn R WAR R
Other ranks 140
Missing other ranks 14

There are no known contemporary accounts that have survived from the soldiers of the 1/7 Royal Warwicks who fought in the Battle of Broodseinde. However, usefully, there is an account from Captain Charles Carrington of the 1/5 Royal Warwicks, which was originally recorded by the BBC in 1964.

As part of the 48th (South Midland) Division, his unit was also involved in the battle and held their positions, alongside the 1/7 Royal Warwicks. Charles Carrington's account of the battle broadly reflects the above war diary entry and he clearly experienced the same conditions within a few hundred yards of the 1/7. His recollections must therefore be the best opportunity to understand what the men experienced over the three days they were in the field. Of course, as Charles Carrington himself acknowledged, individual soldiers may well have felt differently to him. Though the experience itself was a collective one, the individual's reaction to that scenario was entirely personal. That said, his account of the harrowing effects of intense fighting, followed by three days of sitting in mud and water while being shelled, brings disturbing clarity to illustrating the

Captain Charles Carrington. (*Public domain*)

conditions that all of the men had to endure at that end of the battle line. His recollections are therefore highly relevant to this work.

An excerpt transcribed by the author from Captain Carrington's recollections is reproduced below:

By the time it got to the Battle of Passchendaele, I was, as soldiers went, a pretty old soldier. I'd already been through the Somme and I'd been through the very bad winter of 16–17. Which, among other things was the hardest winter for twenty years and was very tough in the trenches. And I was not in very good shape at all in the spring of 1917. And I feel that, even before this Battle of Passchendaele started, I was getting somewhere near the end of my tether. I don't think I could go on much longer.

Every soldier, I suppose, had this breaking strain and when I look back on myself, I see that I was getting near it before this final test came. And then I got into what proved to be the toughest assignment I ever had in my war service, which was the battle of the 4th of October at Passchendaele, when I was commanding a front-line company.

Well, we advanced, just like those battles, under an enormous barrage. A much heavier barrage than I had ever heard before. We ran into a lot of Germans and we had a lot of very severe fighting in the first five minutes, in which I myself got mixed up in a really awkward shooting out affair. Rather like gangsters shooting it out on a western film. However, we shot it out and we won that little battle and we got through and I found that all the various sections of my company had all, in turn, run up against little parties of Germans like that and had fought it out in the shell holes at very close range. And by the time we'd got to our objective, I found that my company was completely scattered. Both my officers, all my sergeants and three quarters of my men were killed or wounded. And there was me and the sergeant major and a scattered handful of men, which we had to get together somehow. Well, we got them together somehow and we settled down on our objective in a group of shell holes and there we sat for three days. And on the second day, it began to rain and rained continuously so that the bog of Passchendaele spread out into a lake. And to begin with, we were sitting up to our knees in mud and water, in rather late autumn, very short of sleep and having just been through this very severe mental strain of the battle itself. And it was after this, there was no further fighting. The Germans did not in fact counter attack us at that point. They were very quick to counter attack in that battle and we had to be on the lookout for it all the time.

However, they shelled us very scientifically and on the second and third days, we just sat in the mud being very heavily and very systematically shelled with pretty heavy stuff. Mostly, the big shells that they used most from their 150mm guns which we called 'five nines'. Well, you could hear these shells coming. They took, I suppose, it's very difficult to say, five or six seconds perhaps to come. And, in, five or six seconds, you can pass through quite a number of psychological changes. Your mind can get through various phases and I don't know whether it is possible to describe the mental changes that one went through.

All day long, one had nothing to do but to sit in the mud, shivering, wet and cold, with no hot food, very short of sleep and having been really rather shattered by the fighting of the previous day. I mean, mentally shattered by it, and try to keep up appearances in some way or another as the shells arrived. They weren't very frequent. There was generally one just arriving and another one just beginning. And when a shell arrived, it would plump into the mud, ten or twenty yards away, or fifty or one hundred yards away and would throw out a burst with a shattering shock which always upset me very much. I've always been very much upset by noise. I hate noise and the noise of the explosions was always a great burden and pain to me. And after it had burst, the splinters of the shell flew off. All of them good killing splinters and might fly twenty, thirty, fifty yards away from the point of impact. And they would take another second or two before they'd all settle down in the mud. And although a shell had burst fifty yards away, you might find one second later, a fragment of jagged iron, nearly red hot and weighing half a pound, arriving in your shell hole.

Well, you'd no sooner managed one than the next one began to appear and you'd hear in the distance, quite a mild pop, as the gun fired, five miles away. And then a humming sound as it approached you through the air, with a noise rather like an aeroplane coming, growing louder and louder. And, as it grew nearer you begin to calculate with yourself whether this one has got your name on it, or not. Well, we were always told that you never heard the shell that hit you. And I think this is probably true because most of them travelled faster than sound. And therefore, if you heard it, it probably wasn't going to be a direct hit on you, but it might be going to fall twenty or thirty yards away from you and be a great danger.

We thought, we pretended, to get very expert in the sounds of shells and the old soldiers thought they knew exactly when they were in great danger and when they weren't. But, I have really some doubts whether they were as clever as they thought they were. I think one could easily be misled about this. The noise would grow into a great crescendo and it would suddenly get louder and louder, until it was like the roar of an aeroplane coming into land on the tarmac. And, at a certain point, your nerve would break and you would throw yourself down in the mud and cringe in the mud till it was past.

When you were listening to this sound of the shells coming over, every now and again there would be one which you made sure was coming very close indeed. The noise would get louder and louder and the machine would seem to accelerate, until it was making a great roar, like an aeroplane coming into land on the tarmac. And there would come a point at which your resolution would break. You would say, this is one for me. And in this flash of time, in the fifth of a second, you'd decide that this is the one and you'd throw yourself down into the mud and cringe into the bottom of the shell hole. And then all the other people around do the same. Well, you may save your life by doing that. But sometimes, you miscalculate and this is a shell that isn't for you at all, but it goes sailing busily on and plunks down on somebody else, three or four hundred yards away. Then you get up and roar with laughter and the other ones who laugh at you for having been the first one to throw yourself down. And this of course is hysterics.

It becomes a kind of game, in which you cling on and try not to let the tension break. And the first person, in a group, who shows the sign of fear, by giving way and taking cover, he's lost a point. And it counts against him. And the one who holds out longest, has gained a point. But in what game? What is this for? Now, this is the problem that I am still unable to solve. That after this long time and after I'd been eighteen months in France and had been through several big battles, that I was still trying to pretend to be brave and not succeeding very well and so were we all.

The thing is a social experience. Not an individual experience. And, speaking for myself, I was always very much more frightened if I was alone in one of these situations, than if I was in a group. But I've heard other soldiers say exactly the opposite. That would be a matter of individual temperament. But I, in trying to reconstruct these extraordinary experiences, I think of it always in terms of what one must call "Esprit de Corps," because there is no other name for it. Unless one is to call it "ganging up." Here we were, a gang of boys, who were committed to this extraordinary range of activities and had to go through with it and all the time one was saying to oneself, "if they can take it, I can take it."

Now, you struggle with these stresses which were almost overpowering and which may become quite overpowering, which may break you down in hysterics. And of course, anybody who remembers battle scenes remembers occasions when someone did go off into a complete mental breakdown and hysterical fits of various sorts, which the doctors eventually admitted and called – described as shell shock.

But there were ways in which you could maintain your self-control. And there is some strange connection between small, physical actions – if you hum a little tune to yourself and feel that you can quietly get through this tune before the next explosion. It gives you a sort of curious feeling of safety. Or you start drumming with your fingers on your knee and have a quite irrational desire to complete this little ritual. These minute things protect you from the nervous collapse, which may come at any moment. But then suddenly, the nervous collapse does come. And there comes the moment when a shell is right on top of you. Then you break, completely and cringe on the ground in a most undignified attitude. After which, you've got to pull yourself up together and start again.

The awful thing being that this is not an isolated experience, but it goes on continuously. Minute after minute and even hour after hour. And in this particular experience, which was the worst that I happened to go through, it went on pretty well continuously for about thirty-six hours. All day and not quite so bad at night. But then, at night it was very cold and wet and you very much wished you were somewhere else than sitting in the dark in the mud.

Then at last, this rather drastic experience came to an end. And somehow or another, we extricated ourselves from the mud and drew back to an extremely uncomfortable camp on the other side of the Ypres canal bank and then we had to count the cost. Now, where do we go from there?

Now, I suppose I might have said this was the point where I would start a revolution or a mutiny, or decide not to do it again. Or something of that kind, as they did in some of the other armies. We didn't take it that way at all. And we had no sooner withdrawn ourselves from this shambles and got together what we could than we began to build up the regiment again and get ready for the next time. And this seems to me extremely difficult to explain. Now, I had lost both my officers and all my sergeants and two thirds of my men. And here I was, I was twenty years old, a young, acting captain and I had to begin to form a new company.

Well, to begin with, I was in a state of complete physical and mental prostration. And I think for a few days after the battle, I was very near having a nervous breakdown. But, when one is young, physical rest very quickly puts that right and in quite a few days, I was almost as good as ever. This seems to me very strange. And I had to begin by actually collecting and organising the men and finding out what had happened to those that had been killed and those who'd been wounded. I had to write twenty-two personal letters to the wives and mothers of men in my company who'd been killed. I then had to choose privates whom I was going to make into corporals, and lance corporals who I was going to make into sergeants at one jump to start again. And then we got a draught of a hundred very good men up from the base. The we started all over again and had a new company. And at the end of a month, we were

ready to do it again. And this seems to me the strangest thing of all when I look back on it. This is one of the things I find hardest to explain.
     Author's transcript of Captain Charles Carrington's interview for the
                                                                    BBC, 1964.

Ultimately, the fighting to capture the ridges and Passchendaele itself carried on after the Battle of Broodseinde, with several more large-scale attacks being launched against the German positions. Finally, British and allied forces achieved their objectives and the village of Passchendaele itself fell to the 1st and 2nd Canadian Divisions on 6 November. A final action on 10 November ensured that the remaining high ground, on Hill 52, north of the village, was captured by a further Canadian assault.

The Great War has produced so many sad ironies and many of the stories of its great battles also produce a sense of outrage and disbelief to this day. Both from the point of view of questionable tactics, General Staff incompetence or intransigence and the staggering loss of life involved. Unfortunately, the Battle of Passchendaele is no exception.

While it is true that the campaign was a great success for the Allied forces, its great sadness is the fact that it may have cost up to 800,000 casualties from both sides. That figure itself is a high-end estimate and the true figures are still unknown and likely to remain so. What is known is that for all that slaughter, all the Allied gains that were made over the campaign were reversed in months, when the Germans launched the Spring Offensive of 1918 and recaptured the very ground taken at such terrible cost.

Chapter 5

On the Ground in October 1917

Ｂy the time the 1/7 Royal Warwicks were ready to go into battle on 4 October, they were a very different unit to the one that had left Coventry in August 1914. Now, rather than being mostly made up of men from Coventry and its surrounding areas, its ranks were filled with men from many different parts of Great Britain and beyond too.

On the eve of the Battle of Broodseinde, the battalion had lost a total of 294 men killed since landing in France in 1915. Though no exact figure is available, they would also have lost many more than that number as wounded. A significant number of these would have been so badly wounded that they would either require long-term treatment and rehabilitation, or never be fit to return to duty again. Consequently, all of these dead and wounded needed to be replaced in order to maintain the fighting efficiency of the unit. Thus, as the casualties mounted, the battalion demographic steadily began to change.

There was, of course, still a significant core of Coventry men serving with the battalion in October 1917. However, replacement of combat losses meant that men were drawn from wherever they happened to be available. They came from such sources as the army reserve, other unit reserves and from conscription and voluntary enlistment, straight off the street and into the battalions. Though, by this time, local recruiting didn't necessarily mean that men were allocated to their local units. It was more that they filled gaps where needed. As will be evidenced shortly, men were therefore routinely transferred between city and county units – many with no local connection at all to their new posting. The result was that one could likely walk the length of a trench occupied by the battalion and hear many different regional and national accents.

The month of October 1917 and more particularly, the Battle of Broodseinde, would see a further 63 men killed in the service of the battalion. Analysis of the list of men killed suggests that all of those killed that month were either as a direct result of the battle, or they died on 8 October – the day after they were withdrawn from the field.

In relation to 8 October, it is not clear just why so many men are listed as dying that day. It is known that the battalion provided men for working parties on that day. However, according to CWGC figures, the battalion lost a total of 30 men over the course of the three-day action, four of whom died in hospital during that period. Yet, the number of men listed as dying on that day is recorded as being twenty-nine. Of which, only one man died in hospital. This means that, of the men declared as dying that day, twenty-eight died in the field.

Such a number is quite high to attribute to deaths on a working party in any one day. Yet, no account exists in either the battalion war diary, the brigade war diary, or any of the diaries of the rest of the brigade units to explain why this may be.

As listed in the previous chapter, the total listed in the war diary of twenty-five men killed during the battle is broadly in accordance with the CWGC data. It also lists a total of fourteen ORs as missing, indicating that the figures given in the diary are as a result of an up-to-date revision to the battalion nominal role. Therefore, a possible explanation may be that the total of missing men has been added to a further fourteen men who were killed after returning to the front on work parties.

After 8 October, only a further four men are recorded as dying during the rest of the month. These are the only deaths the battalion incurred prior to its departure for Italy, in November. All of these men died in hospital, the latest being on 25 October at Rouen, far away from the front. All four of these

Stretcher-bearers evacuating a casualty across Flanders mud. (*Public domain*)

men were buried in cemeteries that served the hospitals they were treated in. However, a closer look at the CWGC figures reveal that, of the 63 men killed, only eleven have known graves. Of those eleven, most are hospital burials. Only three are men who were subsequently recovered from the battlefield and laid to rest. Of which, the identity of one is not entirely certain. Consequently, this means that there are a further 52 men, who still have no known resting place.

For those men who did receive a formal burial, they entered a highly efficient casualty treatment and evacuation system that began on the front line with stretcher-bearers and ended with treatment at hospital. In between, there were dressing stations, casualty clearing stations (CCSs), ambulances and light railways, all dedicated to the treatment and, if needed, the evacuation of the wounded.

Dressing stations and CCSs were located close to the front line and two of the men who died of wounds were buried in cemeteries established to serve CCSs. These cemeteries are Mendinghem and Dozinghem, which, along with Bandaghem, were named by the troops as a play on words for genuine local place names, such as the village of Lozinghem, in northern France. Both Mendinghem (mending them) and Dozinghem (dosing them) are cemeteries that served CCSs located to the northwest of Ypres and Poperinghe.

After the war, with so many medical aid posts establishing their own cemeteries, the areas of the old battlefields were dotted with smaller burial grounds. These were added to by those bodies recovered from the field, either during or after action by burial parties and laid to rest close to where they fell, often in small unit-specific cemeteries. Many of these smaller plots were subsequently 'concentrated' into much larger cemeteries, where men were exhumed from the smaller locations. They were then re-interred in bigger cemeteries, such as Poelcapelle British Cemetery and Tyne Cot. It is at Tyne Cot cemetery where, like the Thiepval Memorial to the missing of the Somme and the Menin Gate Memorial at Ypres, the 63 men of the 1/7 Royal Warwicks are remembered on the vast memorial wall. This commemorates the names of almost 35,000 officers and men who were lost during the fighting around Ypres but who have no known grave.

In the following chapter, the lives of the men who fought and died in October 1917 will be examined as much as is possible, in terms of the information available and the time allowed to research them. The hope is that, in some small way, the names of just a small group of Great War soldiers will become something more than a name on a memorial once more. As a result, their stories will be preserved alongside that of their comrades, and their sacrifice and that of their families will be more fully appreciated.

The enormous sweep of a section of the memorial wall at Tyne Cot Cemetery, where the names of nearly 35,000 missing soldiers are commemorated. (*Author's photo*)

Some of the accounts are very brief and others are more detailed where more extensive information has been available. The stories of their lives have been teased out of many different sources of information, such as a number of military databases, service records, census returns and birth, marriage and death registrations to name but a few. Much information has also been

Affectionately referred to as Pip, Squeak and Wilfred, the 1914–15 Star, The British War Medal and Victory Medal. As issued to all servicemen who saw active service from 1914 onwards, these medals were awarded to all the men of the 1/7 Royal Warwicks who saw active service prior to 31 December 1915. Those entering active service afterwards did not receive the star. (*Author's collection*)

obtained from the many local history societies and commemorative and historical websites set up to remember these men, the units they served in and the battles they fought.

They tell of men from many different backgrounds and places. There are accounts of successes, tragedies, heroism, love and pride. Included too are the details of how their government sought to compensate their loved ones for their loss. This last inclusion is important, as it leads to the sobering realisation that, in each case, the only thing left for their families was just a small amount of money and the plaques and medals bestowed by a grateful nation. Most often in lieu of a final, known resting place. Perhaps, in that regard, it is fitting to remember the words of a father who addressed his fallen son's university, sometime after the war. His words simplified the famous line from Laurence Binyon's poem 'For the Fallen', which said: *'They shall grow not old, as we that are left grow old'.*

That father's own version of that famous line was simply:

'They not only sacrificed everything they had, they sacrificed everything they were to become.'

Chapter 6
The Fallen

Cap badge of the Royal Warwickshire Regiment. (*Author's collection*)

In honour of the fallen

1/7 Bn (TF) The Royal Warwickshire Regiment

Who gave their lives at
The Battle of Broodseinde, fought near Poelcapelle, 4–7 October 1917

The Glorious Dead

They shall grow not old
As we that are left grow old
Age shall not weary them
Nor the years condemn
At the going down of the sun
And in the morning
We will remember them

Frederick George Bailey – Sergeant 265740

Killed in action on 8 October 1917, aged 26 years.
Commemorated at Tyne Cot Memorial.
Panel 24A.

Frederick Bailey was born on 6 May 1891 in Great Wakering, a village just a few miles from Southend, in Essex. Brother to Walden, Elizabeth, Thomas and Harold, he was the eldest son of George, a carpenter and joiner by trade, and mother, Helena.

Census information from 1901 indicates that the family trade was construction. It also records that George and Helena were resident at 26, High Street, Great Wakering with George's father, Thomas, a widower who is listed as a builder and employer. Presumably, it was Thomas providing a livelihood for George and his young family as well as a roof above their heads.

By the time of the 1911 Census, Frederick was 21 years old and working as a draper's assistant. He had also moved out of the family home and was by then living in lodgings in South Street, Eastbourne with a number of other workers employed in the same trade.

It is unclear when Frederick moved from Eastbourne. However, at the outbreak of war, he had taken up residence in Leamington Spa, Warwickshire. In the September after war was declared, he enlisted with the 1/7 Royal Warwicks at Coventry. It is therefore highly likely that Frederick would have either shipped to France when the battalion first entered the Western Front theatre of operations in March 1915, or very soon afterwards as part of an early reinforcement party.

Although Frederick died in action, his death did not occur during the Battle of Broodseinde. Instead, he was killed the day after the battalion had been relieved from their positions and was by then located at Siege Farm camp, just west of the Yser Canal. Despite having just completed three days of fighting in appalling conditions, the battalion was still required to provide men for working parties back out on the battlefield. It was to be in one of those working parties that Frederick would meet his death in the most tragic of circumstances.

Frederick had volunteered to lead a small working party out into no man's land and during that task he had been severely wounded. He was eventually located by stretcher-bearers who, during the process of trying to get Frederick back to safety, were themselves caught up in enemy shelling of the area. Just as they had reached the apparent safety of British lines, a shell burst overhead, killing Frederick and one of the stretcher-bearers and wounding the other.

It is unknown whether Frederick received a burial in the field. But, if he did, his grave was subsequently lost, hence his inclusion on the memorial to the missing at Tyne Cot.

Because he never married, his effects of money and savings amounting to £24.19/9d were paid to his mother, Helena. She also later received a war gratuity of £16.10/- and a dependant's pension of 5/- a week, payable from 16 April 1919.

Frederick is remembered in his home village of Great Wakering, both on a wooden memorial plaque located in St Nicholas's Church and on the village war memorial erected in the form of a stone cross outside the church.

St Nicholas Parish Church and war memorial cross, Great Wakering.
(*Photo credit – C. Churchman. War Memorials Online*)

Herbert John Ellard Barnes – Private 266703

Killed in action on 4 October 1917, aged 29 years.
Commemorated at Tyne Cot Memorial.
Panel 24.

Herbert Barnes was born in December 1888, the first son of his carpenter father, James and mother, Mary. Home at that time was 87, King Street, Leamington Spa, where his first brother, James, was born around three years later. Herbert's second brother, Edward, was born when he was about 14 years of age.

The 1911 Census records a 22-year-old Herbert still living at home and working as a house painter. Though he would soon leave home and in 1913 Herbert married Ethel Freer, a 21-year-old laundry maid, also from Leamington Spa. In the August of that year, their first child, Lavinia, was born.

The couple had settled down with Ethel's family at 36, Charles Street and it was in the late spring of 1915, when Ethel was pregnant once more, that Herbert decided to enlist.

On 25 May, he enlisted at Leamington Spa and became Gunner 655 Barnes of the Warwickshire Royal Horse Artillery (RHA), a territorial unit. Because he was attested and embodied with his unit that day, he went straight into training. His son, Herbert, was born the following month.

On 18 December of that year, Herbert was transferred to the 1/7 Royal Warwicks as Private 4693, where he subsequently completed his training. He remained in England until 7 March 1916, when he joined the battalion that were by then posted to the front line, close to the village of Foncquevillers.

It seems that, during his time on the front line, Herbert did not enjoy the best of health. In July 1916 he was wounded, possibly while taking part in a trench raid on enemy positions. At the time the battalion was occupying trenches around La Boiselle. Though the nature of his injury is not known, it is recorded that he was 'wounded at duty', which essentially means that he sustained a minor wound that would have been treated locally, without the need for medical evacuation from the front.

At Eclusiers on 9 February 1917, Herbert was admitted to a CCS, having come down with a fever, but returned to duty on the twenty-second of that month. However, he was again admitted to hospital on 12 May 1917, first to No.2 General Hospital at Le Havre, via No.5 CCS and then on to No.12 General Hospital at Rouen. Apparently, Herbert had been on a work party unloading trucks at the Peronne railhead when he strained himself and sustained an inguinal hernia. Though requiring hospital treatment, the injury was not deemed serious in nature and he subsequently returned to duty the following July.

Though Herbert was granted ten days' leave in the September of 1917, this was only field leave. He therefore never got the opportunity to return home to see his young family once more and was killed in action and his body lost on 4 October – the first day of the Broodseinde offensive.

Herbert's widow, Ethel, received a war gratuity of £10.10/- and a pension of 22/11d a week, which was an enhanced payment to take into account his two children. In 1920 Ethel married a local man by the name of William Eales and appears to have lived the rest of her life in Warwick, where she subsequently passed away in 1969, aged 77 years.

As well as being commemorated on the memorial wall at Tyne Cot cemetery, Herbert is also remembered on the war memorial erected in Euston Place, Leamington Spa and in the parish church of St John the Baptist, Leamington Priors.

Sidney Alfred Batt – Private 300007

Killed in action on 4 October 1917, aged 18 years.
Believed to be buried at Tyne Cot Cemetery.
Grave reference: IX. G. 6.

Sidney Batt was born in the last quarter of 1899 in Chelsea, London. At the time of the 1901 Census, the Batt family home was 8, St Marks Road, Brompton, in the borough of Kensington, London. His father, William Batt, was a labourer, while his mother, Ellen, was also caring for his elder siblings: William, Nellie and Albert.

By the 1911 Census, the family had moved to a modest-sized home in Warbury Road, Chelsea and Sidney's father had found work as a house painter. His eldest brother, William, was by then 18 and working in the same trade as his father, presumably alongside him. By this time, Sidney had also acquired a younger brother, Edward, who was eight at the time of the census.

No service record exists for Sidney, so there is no background information as to his trade or address when he enlisted. However, it is known that he enlisted at Wandsworth around March 1916 and was initially Private 13306 of the East Surrey Regiment. We can also surmise that, due to his age when he died, he had lied about his age in order to be able to fight.

Just as with much of the detail relating to his life, Sidney's death also poses certain mysteries. Although it is known that he fell in action on 4 October, it would appear that his body remained undiscovered until post-war body recovery teams were working in the area to find the fallen. As can be seen from the headstone bearing Sidney's details, it carries the inscription 'believed to be' at the head of the stone. It is therefore not actually certain that the remains in that particular grave are that of Sidney.

The reason for this doubt is that when the remains were recovered from the battlefield, the only means of identification present was a mess tin, which had been inscribed with Sidney's service number. Consequently, without the certainty provided by the presence of more personal items, such as pay books, identity tags and personal correspondence carried by the soldier, there must have been a reluctance to say conclusively that the remains found were actually Sidney's. After all, it is entirely possible that another soldier could have retrieved Sidney's mess tin to replace his own and had then been killed later. Sadly, we will therefore never know the truth behind the very last chapter of Sidney's story.

Headstone of the grave believed to contain the remains of Private Sidney Batt. Tyne Cot Cemetery. (*Author's photo*)

Sidney's mother, Ellen, was designated his sole legatee and she subsequently received his savings of £3.13/.6d. She also received a war gratuity of £9.10/- and a weekly pension of 5/-.

The whereabouts of any local war memorials where Sidney is commemorated are currently unknown.

John Stanley Beard – Private 266755

Died of wounds on 5 October 1917, aged 25 years.
Buried at Abbeville Communal Cemetery Extension.
Grave reference: III. C. 22.

Headstone inscription reads:

WELL DONE GOOD AND FAITHFUL SERVANT
ENTER THOU INTO THE JOY OF THY LORD

John Beard enlisted for service at No.3 Recruiting Office, Curzon Hall, Suffolk Street, Birmingham on 10 December 1915. However, it would not be until 8 February 1916 that the then 23-year-old John, a draper by profession, was called up for service with the Colours and attested as Private 4756 of the 1/7 Royal Warwicks.

Born in Hereford in 1892, John was living at 17, Avondale Road, Sparkhill, Birmingham, with his parents: Michael, a painter and decorator, and his mother, Marian. Prior to becoming a draper, he had worked in a drapers warehouse and presumably learnt his trade there. John also had two brothers: Michael, two years his senior and Henry, who was eight years older. However, Henry is not listed as a sibling on John's service record, which may suggest he died in childhood.

On 30 August 1916, John landed in France and joined his battalion, which were by then engaged in extended training around the area of Bois de Warnemont. Unfortunately, all we know about his service before his death is that John had been appointed acting lance corporal the previous month but had reverted to the rank of private upon joining his unit.

On 5 October 1917, John was badly wounded and evacuated from the front. However, he was never to make it to hospital and succumbed to his wounds on No.11 Ambulance Train later that day.

Because John had not been lost on the battlefield, the army was able to send his personal effects home to his parents and that list of items perhaps tells us a lot more about John than anything recorded in official records. Those items were:

His identity disc, some letters and postcards. Photos, a flash lamp and a metal ring. A metal cigarette case with a pipe, tobacco pouch and a cigarette holder in a case. A fountain pen filler and eye glasses in a case. There was also a knife, some scissors, five pencils, a penny stamp, a badge and a metal mirror. Lastly, he was carrying a black bead rosary, a prayer book and a copy of the Gospel of St John.

John's parents, Michael and Marian, were listed as joint legatees to John's monetary effects and received his savings of £3.18/15d and a war gratuity of £7.00. Michael was later awarded a weekly war pension of 7/6d.

The location of any local war memorial bearing his name is unknown at this time.

William Beech – Private 267510 "B" Coy

Died on 8 October 1917, aged 32 years.
Commemorated at Tyne Cot Memorial.
Panel 25A.

Older brother to twins Fred and Arthur and his youngest sibling, Walter, William Beech was born in Birmingham in 1885. The 1891 and 1901 Census records show that William and his family were initially living in the Aston area of the city, before moving to 81, Avondale Road in Sparkhill, which was the family address at the time of the 1911 Census.

William's mother, Emma, was from Birmingham. While his father, also William, hailed from Newport, Salop and worked as a blacksmith. Indeed, metalworking was a trade that all of the Beech men were engaged in by 1911, save for Walter, who was only 13 at the time and still in school.

It appears that as soon as William was old enough to work, he had followed his father into the metalworking industry – his first recorded job being as an Oliver smith. This role was a skilled occupation, requiring the smith to operate a hammer called an Oliver, powered either by a treadle or motor and used to drop forge small items such as nails and bolts. It is likely a skill he was still utilising when his last trade of producing window fittings was listed in the 1911 census.

As with many of the soldiers whose names appear in this work, William's service record no longer exists. Consequently, although we can say that he enlisted in Birmingham, we can only say that this is likely to have been in the months following 9 October 1916. This being roughly calculated using available war gratuity information. Though this does indicate that he had probably enlisted by the time he wed his fiancée, Julia (nee Hamilton), who had formerly been employed as a press operator. The couple married in Birmingham in the last quarter of 1916.

William was killed on 8 October and available records state only that his death was 'presumed', indicating that nobody could say for certain what actually happened to him that day. As his sole legatee, Julia received William's savings of £5.5/10d, a war gratuity of £3.00 and a widow's pension of 13/9d a week. This enhanced pension payment would indicate that the couple probably had at least one child.

William's widow married again and remained in Birmingham. She was living at 6, Colmore Terrace at the time she became eligible for payment of her widow's pension in July 1918. Later, presumably after marrying again, she moved to 22, Colmore Terrace. Then known as Julia Wright, she passed away in Birmingham in July 1975, aged 82.

William is remembered at Tyne Cot memorial as one of the thousands of British and Commonwealth soldiers whose final resting place is unknown. It is not known if he is commemorated on any local war memorials.

Richard Benny – Private 266525

Killed in action on 4 October 1917, aged 22 years.
Commemorated at Tyne Cot Memorial.
Panel 25A.

Richard Benny was born in the Foleshill area of Coventry around October 1894 and came from a sizeable family. His mother, Sarah, hailed from Staffordshire, while his father, also Richard, came from Fermoy, County Cork, in Ireland. Records show that Richard Snr took on various manual jobs to feed his growing family, such as coal mining and labouring in the ordnance industry.

The 1911 Census records that while Richard, his father and youngest sister, Ada, were still living together, the rest of Richard's siblings had moved out of the family home at 24, Bridge Row, in the Foleshill area of Coventry. The survey also records that Richard's mother, Sarah, had died by then and at 16 years old, Richard was working as a machinist in a cycle works. This was a major industry in Coventry at the time. The only other residents were William and Esther Tevener, a couple from the London area who were boarding with the Bennys.

Richard had two older brothers, George and Arthur, and a younger brother, Percy. As well as Ada, Richard also had three older sisters: Sarah, Florence and Beatrice. Moreover, from Richard's enlistment record, it appears he was actually living with Beatrice at the time as he gave his address as 55, Eden Street. This was Beatrice's home and located just a short distance from his father's house.

Richard enlisted for service, at Coventry, with the 1/7 Royal Warwicks on 7 June 1915 and was originally issued with the service number, 4365. Once his basic training was completed, he joined his unit on 23 February 1916 as part of a draft of forty-nine fresh troops. By then the battalion was stationed in the area of Foncquevillers and had just been relieved in the front line by the 1/8 Royal Warwicks.

The day Richard arrived at the front saw the start of three days of snow fall. Having just been relieved from the trenches, it was now the battalion's turn to provide men for working parties. And so, although not thrown straight into combat, his first taste of life on the Western Front was one of hard toil in bitterly cold conditions. His actual introduction to the front line would come six days later when the snow had thawed and the battalion took over very wet and muddy trenches in L Sector, close to Foncquevillers.

On 16 November 1916, in the closing stages of the Somme campaign, the battalion was engaged in working parties, close to Bazentin le Petit, when Richard sustained a gunshot wound to his right knee. Initially, he was evacuated from the front to No.6 General Hospital in Rouen, via 45 CCS. From there he was evacuated back to a hospital in Liverpool, before moving on to Ballyvonare Convalescent Camp, in Ireland.

After a lengthy period recovering from his wounds, Richard eventually rejoined his unit on 29 June 1917. At the time, the battalion had just been relieved from trenches on the Morchies-Baumetz Line. They then engaged in training, having been posted to Bedford Camp, close to the village of Gomiecourt and located a few miles to the north west of Bapaume. This training would continue for another month, until the battalion finally moved up into the Flanders region for the start of the Third Battle of Ypres on 31 July 1917.

As fate would have it, Richard was wounded again on 17 August 1917, receiving a shrapnel wound to the back. He was evacuated from the field by the 1/3 South Midland Field Ambulance (SMFA) and passed to a nearby CCS. However, by the twenty-fourth of that month, he was returned fit to his unit and recommenced combat duties in that sector.

Had his wound been a little more serious, perhaps he may not have been present for the attack on the morning of 4 October, convalescing instead well away from the front. This, however, was not to be and Richard was killed in action on the first day of the attack.

As his sole beneficiary, Richard's father received payment of his son's savings of £7.15/7d. He was also paid a war gratuity of £10.00. However, his subsequent claim for a dependant's war pension was eventually refused in October 1925.

Although commemorated on the memorial wall at Tyne Cot, it is not known if Richard is commemorated on any local memorials.

Albert Bird – Private 19091

Died on 4 October 1917, aged 19 years.
Commemorated at Tyne Cot Memorial.
Panel 25A.

If a person's life leaves its own footprint in history, then Albert Bird's was a very faint impression indeed. What is known is that he was born to John Bird, a polisher, and his mother, Rose (nee Atkins), in Hockley, Birmingham

Bronze memorial plaque inside St Edburgha's parish church, Yardley, Birmingham. Private Albert Bird's name appears in column two of the lower panel. (*Author's photo*)

on 20 March 1898. The following April, he was baptised at All Saints Parish Church, also in Hockley.

At the time of his birth, the young family were resident at 6, Turners Buildings, Park Road, Hockley. However, the 1901 Census seems to be the last time Albert appears in official records. By then he was three years old and living with Rose and her parents, William and Sarah Atkins, at 179, Park Grove, again in Hockley. Resident there too was Rose's younger sister, Lucy. Interestingly, there is no mention of Albert's father, John.

We do know that Albert enlisted around September to October 1916 at Birmingham and was by then a resident of the South Yardley area of the city. Though, with no surviving service record to refer to, there is very little else that can be said about his life.

Albert fell in battle on 4 October and it was Rose who was his sole legatee, receiving £2.14/2d in savings and a war gratuity of £5.10/-. It appears she was awarded a war pension but no details are held on the surviving record card, so we cannot say where she was living, or how much she was awarded for her loss.

As one of the missing, Albert is commemorated at Tyne Cot cemetery. His name is also included on the striking bronze memorial plaque in St Edburgha's parish church, Yardley, dedicated to the men of the parish who fell in the Great War.

Joseph Samuel Bowley – Private 300099

Died on 8 October 1917, aged 34 years.
Commemorated at Tyne Cot Memorial.
Panel 25A.

Born in October 1882, Joseph Bowley is one of a number of the battalion's men killed during October 1917 who was a good deal older than the average casualty of that time.

Initially a resident of the Ladywood area of Birmingham, Joseph's early years were spent at the family home in 163, St Vincent Street. His father, also Joseph Samuel, was an iron bedstead caster and his mother, Jane, originally hailed from Wolverhampton.

When Joseph became old enough to earn a living, he followed in his father's footsteps and took up the trade of bedstead casting, or dressing. Had the information from the 1901 Census been available, then a fuller picture of the family's life would have been gained from the census of that year. Unfortunately, though, this information has so far proven elusive and a significant gap therefore exists in Joseph's story.

However, by the time of the 1911 Census, Joseph was head of his own household. Having married Agnes Louisa (nee Corbett) in Aston, in 1903, they were by then the parents of six-year-old Grace, four-year-old Joseph and their youngest child, Frank, who was just one year old at the time. Home for the family was 8, Peel Street, a two-up, two-down house in the Winson Green area of Birmingham. This was just a short distance from the old Bowley family home in Ladywood and very much a working-class area.

Because Joseph's service record no longer exists, it is not possible to say exactly when he enlisted, though we do know that it took place in Birmingham, probably in the month following 9 September 1916. Joseph initially joined the Norfolk Regiment (The Norfolks) as Private 7287, though the date of his subsequent transfer to 1/7 Royal Warwicks is unknown.

Joseph was subsequently killed in action on 8 October 1917. As his widow and sole legatee, Agnes received his total savings of £2.9/-. She also received a war gratuity of £3.10/- and a widow's pension. Though the pension record did not say how much Agnes received, it did reveal evidence of a further family tragedy, as it records that there were only two dependant children in the family. This clearly meant that one of Joseph and Agnes's children had died since the 1911 Census. A subsequent retrospective examination of the relevant records revealed that the child in question was Frank, who died in April 1911.

As one of the missing, Joseph's name is included on the memorial wall at Tyne Cot. It is not known if he is commemorated on any local war memorials.

John Welch Bradshaw – Corporal 265706

Killed in action on 4 October 1917, aged 32 years.
Commemorated at Tyne Cot Memorial.
Panel 24.

John Bradshaw was the youngest of five children born to farmer Henry Bradshaw and his wife, Annis (nee Welch). Of the siblings, the eldest was his sister Edith, eleven years his senior, followed by Alice, seven years older, then Ellen, who was six years older. Finally, his brother, William, preceded him by four years. Early life for the Bradshaw children was spent on the family farm in the village of Offchurch, which lies just a few miles to the east of Leamington Spa.

John was born in the July of 1884 and at the time of the 1891 Census, the family was still living on the farm and Henry, at 54 years old, was still active as a farmer. Although, by the time of the 1901 Census, Henry had retired and sold up and the family had moved to 4, Forfield Place, a well-appointed Victorian terraced house, not far from the centre of Leamington Spa. This move certainly indicates that the family were relatively well off, given that they were then living in a fairly well-to-do middle-class area of the town.

By then, all of John's siblings were working. Edith and Alice had their own millinery business, William was an agent for a cattle food company and John himself had been taken on as a fine art apprentice. Another resident of the Bradshaw family home was Eleann Hearn, a 65-year-old spinster who was boarding with the family and wealthy enough to live off her own means. The youngest sister, Ellen, who would have been around 22 at the time, does not appear as resident in the family home.

It seems that the Bradshaw family enjoyed a good deal of success in their ventures. By the time the 1911 Census had rolled around, William had taken a wife, Margaret, and John, still a bachelor, was living with the couple. Home was a house called Sunnyside, a spacious eight-roomed house on the Warwick

Kenilworth town war memorial, which stands at the top of Abbey Fields. (*Author's photo*)

Road, Kenilworth. At that time, both William and John were engaged in commercial travelling. An occupation that seemed to provide all of them with a very comfortable existence.

As with so many of the soldiers written about in this work. John's service record no longer exists. There is therefore no way of filling in that gap between census and enlistment, which would have told us a little more about his life prior to army service. We can only say that John subsequently enlisted around May 1915 at Coventry and that his life ended on 4 October, when he was reportedly shot by a German sniper.

After his death, his savings were divided among his siblings with payments of £1.14/3d going to William and Edith and payments of £1.14/2d for Alice and Ellen. However, it would be William, the older brother, who would receive a war gratuity payment of £14.10/-. Though, disappointingly, no pension record could be found for him.

Today, as well as at Tyne Cot, John's name is commemorated on Kenilworth's war memorial. Sited at the top of Abbey Fields, the memorial looks down towards Warwick Road. Not so very far away from the location of Sunnyside, the house he once shared with William and Margaret.

Paul Bradshaw – Private 268604

Died of wounds on 4 October 1917, aged 40 years.
Commemorated at Tyne Cot Memorial.
Panel 25.

Very few records remain to tell us about Paul Bradshaw's early years. Nothing is known about his parents, save that his mother's maiden name was Cotterill. There is also no record of where the family lived, or if Paul had any siblings. At this time, we can only say that he was born in Edgbaston, Birmingham in the first quarter of 1877.

The next time Paul appears on record is in 1898 when, on 30 July, he married Jane Dugmore at St Patrick's Church, Dudley Road, Birmingham. The couple does not then appear again until the 1911 Census records them as living in four-room accommodation at 88, Winson Street, just off Dudley Road in the Winson Green area of Birmingham. Paul was by then employed as a silversmith and Jane was also working in the jewellery trade as a scratch brusher.

The census also records that 22-year-old Kate Dugmore, presumably a younger relation to Jane, was living with the couple as a boarder and was also employed in the jewellery trade as a polisher. With Kate under their roof too, life for the Bradshaws must have been very cramped at the time, given that also sharing their four-room house were their five children: Mary, 11, John, eight, Ellen, two, and three-month-old twins, Paul and Stephen.

Our knowledge of Paul improves considerably come 13 August 1914 – the date when he enlisted at Thorp Street Drill Hall, Birmingham, as Private 2348 of the 5th Bn Royal Warwicks. Fortunately, Paul's service record has survived and it tells us a good deal about his service. Importantly, one of the first things it indicates to us is that Paul was more than eager to do his bit. We know this because, not only had he enlisted just a little more than two weeks after the start of the war, he had also lied about his age.

Much has been said about those young men who, being younger than the minimum age of 19 for active service, had added months and years to their ages to be able to join the fight. Yet less mention is made of those older men who, being either too old to meet the maximum age limit, or being very close to it, chose to lie about their age on enlistment.

Paul was one of these men and at the time he enlisted he was well past his thirty-seventh birthday. He should thus only have seen around a year's service, before reaching the maximum age of 38. Perhaps fearful of rejection, he therefore told the recruiting staff that he was in fact 34, enabling him to sign on for a term of four years.

Paul's basic training seems to have progressed well. So well in fact that he was promoted to substantive (paid) lance corporal on 1 November, less than three months after enlisting. He then entered the Western Front theatre when he, along with the rest of the battalions of the Warwickshire Brigade, sailed for Le Havre, disembarking on 22 March 1915. However, Paul's so far unblemished record ended abruptly on 26 October 1915 with the loss of his rank. At the time, the 1/5 Royal Warwicks were manning front-line trenches at Bayencourt and the battalion war diary and surviving copies of battalion orders give no indication as to why. Moreover, his service record notes only that the demotion was for 'irregular conduct' and that it occurred in the field.

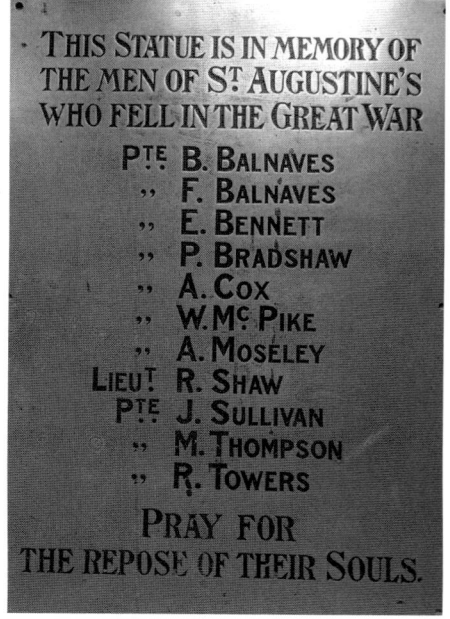

THIS STATUE IS IN MEMORY OF THE MEN OF Sᵗ AUGUSTINE'S WHO FELL IN THE GREAT WAR

PᵀᴱE B. BALNAVES
,,   F. BALNAVES
,,   E. BENNETT
,,   P. BRADSHAW
,,   A. COX
,,   W. Mᶜ PIKE
,,   A. MOSELEY
LIEUᵀ R. SHAW
PᵀE J. SULLIVAN
,,   M. THOMPSON
,,   R. TOWERS

PRAY FOR THE REPOSE OF THEIR SOULS.

The brass memorial plaque, currently in storage at St Augustine's Catholic Church, Handsworth, Birmingham. (*Author's photo*)

Paul served for almost another year with the 1/5 Royal Warwicks, before being posted to the 1/7 Royal Warwicks on 4 October 1916. He arrived at his new unit on 23 October, when the battalion was engaged in a period of training at Sombrin. Though by early November, Paul moved again, this time joining a CCS at Sailly as a stretcher-bearer.

Such arduous work through what was a very harsh winter eventually took its toll on Paul and he eventually became a casualty himself. By 2 February of the following year, he was admitted first to No.12 General Hospital at Rouen with rheumatism and then on to hospital in England. By April, Paul had been transferred to the convalescent facility at Ballyvonare, Co Cork, before returning to England. Here he joined the regimental reserve battalion, at Cramlington, on 3 August 1917.

Paul was eventually returned to the front and rejoined the 1/7 Royal Warwicks in the area of Ypres on 21 September 1917. From then, it would only be another two weeks before Paul died of wounds sustained in battle on 4 October. At 40 years old, along with one other man of the same age, they are the oldest known casualties lost by the battalion during the Broodseince offensive.

It is unknown if Paul received any sort of medical treatment or burial after receiving his wounds. However, given the fact that he has no known grave, it is unlikely that he ever got further than evacuation to a forward aid station, which may only have been able to afford him a hasty burial in ground likely to be torn up by shelling later.

At the time of his death, Paul's widow, Jane, was living at 130, Newcombe Road, Handsworth with children, John, Helen, and the twins, Paul and Stephen, listed as his dependant children. No mention is made of the eldest child, Mary, who would have been around 17 at the time of Paul's death. Her fate therefore remains a mystery at this time. Jane subsequently received Paul's savings of £5.3/10d and a war gratuity of £14.00. She was also awarded a war pension of 33/9d a week.

Paul is remembered on the memorial wall at Tyne Cot and locally on a commemorative plaque to the fallen of the parish. This is now kept in storage at Saint Augustine's Roman Catholic Church, Avenue Road, Handsworth. The church stands just two streets away from the home Paul shared with his family.

John Bromhead – Private 267519

Died of wounds on 17 October 1917
after wounds received on 8 October, aged 27 years.
Buried at St. Sever Cemetery Extension, Rouen.
Grave reference: P. III. J. 10B.

Born in Birmingham in January 1890, John Bromhead was the second son of gas fitter James Frederick (Fred) Bromhead and his wife, Hannah (nee Tudge). The 1901 Census records that older son, Gordon, was two years older than John and that he also had two younger siblings: Kate, who was three at the time and David, who had been born in July of the previous year. At the time, of the census, the family were living at 26, Freeman Street in central Birmingham. Fred was then 42 and Hannah was 40.

Tragedy subsequently befell the family in December 1905. In that month, not only did John's mother, Hannah, die but his youngest sister, Hannah Tudge Bromhead, was born. Though entirely speculation, the coinciding dates for both strongly indicate that Hannah either died in childbirth, or very shortly afterwards. Given that Fred would by then have had to take on the running of the house and the care of the family on his own, it is no surprise that baby Hannah would prove to be too much of a burden. She was therefore adopted and went to live with relatives of Hannah in her birthplace of Pudleston, Herefordshire.

On 23 January 1915, John married Nellie Palmer at Saint Andrew's Church, Bordesley, Birmingham. Home for the newlyweds was 5, Kingston Terrace, off the Coventry Road, Birmingham, with John working as a cellar man. They would enjoy the best part of two years together before John enlisted on 24 June 1916. He was then called up for service as Private 6078 of the 1/7 Royal Warwicks, in Birmingham, on 2 November 1916.

Having completed his basic training, John landed in France on 8 February 1917. However, it does appear that he had been away from the battalion on attachment at some point between then and 7 September 1917, when he rejoined the battalion, by then in the field in the Ypres area.

Having survived the fighting over the three days of the Battle of Broodseinde, John was seriously wounded on 8 October. He managed to survive evacuation from the field and was sent to No.6 General Hospital at Rouen where he finally succumbed to his wounds on 17 October.

John left savings of £3.9/3d. to his widow, Nellie. She also received an initial war gratuity of £5.00 and a pension of 13/9d. a week. A further gratuity of £3.00 was authorised at the end of 1919. It is not known at this time if John's name appears on any local memorials.

Leonard Brown – Private 29299

Died on 4 October 1917, aged 19 years.
Commemorated at Tyne Cot Memorial.
Panel 25.

The youngest of six children, Leonard Brown was born in the parish of St Mary's in Bedford in July 1898.

In the census of 1901, Leonard was just two years old and his eldest siblings, William, then 16, and 12-year-old Christina, were already working as domestic servants. As well as his father, Elisha, a bricklayer's labourer, and his mother, Verina, it was 11-year-old Bertha, ten-year-old Clara and five-year-old Arthur who made up the rest of the family. Home for the Browns at that time was 20, Holme Street, Bedford. Long demolished now, the accommodation was cramped, comprising less than five rooms in total.

Tragedy would soon follow for the Brown family as Elisha died the following year at just 43 years old, leaving William as man of the house. At some stage after the death of his father, William left domestic service and took up labouring. However, in August 1904, he enlisted as Private 7169 Brown in the Lincolnshire Regiment.

For Verina, it would be seven years before her widowhood ended and she married William Banham, a timber yard labourer and three years her junior, in 1909. The 1911 Census shows the family living at 11, St Leonard's Street, in Bedford. A slightly larger six-roomed terraced house, just a couple of hundred yards down the road from their old house in Holme Street. At 26, William by this time, had been discharged from the army and was back at home, working as a mechanic and labourer at a local iron works. Christina was by then 23 and a laundress and also still at home. Fourteen-year-old Arthur had found work as a milk boy and 12-year-old Leonard was still at school. Though by then, he was no longer the youngest child as he now had a younger brother, Horice – the last of Elisha and Verina's children together.

The record makes no mention of Bertha and Clara. However, they would both have been adults by this point and likely either married, or possibly working in a live-in role.

Having been discharged from the Colours in 1907, William was still on the army reserve list when war broke out in 1914. Though, he was discharged from this obligation when he subsequently enlisted with the Canadian Permanent Force and became Private 477118 Brown of the Royal Canadian Regiment. However, on 16 September 1916, tragedy struck the Brown family once more, when William fell in action at the battle of Flers-Courcelette.

Wooden memorial plaque inside St Mary's Church, Bedford. Now no longer accessible to the general public. (*Photo courtesy of Mark Phillips, Albion Archaeology, St Mary's Church, Bedford*)

Leonard was just 18 when he enlisted in January 1917, just four months after the death of his brother. Initially he served as Private 32418 in the Norfolk Regiment and about a month after enlistment, he was in France.

Leonard saw action at Vimy Ridge, close to where his brother had fallen. He also fought in the Passchendaele and Cambrai sectors. However, it is not known when, during his service, he was transferred to the Royal Warwickshire Regiment.

Leonard fell in action on 4 October 1917. Like his brother, his body was never recovered and he has no known grave. His mother, Verina, would receive his savings of £3.11/-, a war gratuity of £3.00 and a dependant's pension of 5/- a week. She passed away, aged 72 years, in March 1931.

Leonard is remembered on the memorial wall at Tyne Cot, just as his brother's name is carved on the Vimy Memorial in France. Both brothers are also remembered on a carved wooden memorial plaque in their home parish church of St Mary's in Bedford. However, St Mary's church itself has now been converted to commercial use and the plaque is no longer accessible to the public.

Arthur William Cusack Butler – Corporal 265323

Died on 8 October 1917, aged 20 years.
Commemorated at Tyne Cot Memorial.
Panel 24.

Arthur William Cusack Butler was born in 1896 and christened at All Saints Parish Church, Emscote, Warwick on 17 December of that year. He was the eldest son of Walter, a painter and decorator, and mother, Susan Ann (nee Plumb). At the time of the 1901 Census, four-year-old Arthur had one older sister, Mabel, who at the time of the census was two years his senior. He also had a baby brother, James, who was just five months old. Home for the Butlers at that time was 123, Emscote Road, Warwick.

By the time of the 1911 Census, the family had moved to the neighbouring town of Leamington Spa and were living at 154, Leam Terrace. By then, the 14-year-old errand boy, Arthur, had acquired three new brothers: John, six, Herbert, five and Walter, three.

Though it is unknown when Arthur enlisted, we can say that this was before the outbreak of the Great War. We know this because Arthur was a recipient of one of the rarest of Great War campaign medals, the Territorial Force War Medal.

Established in 1920, this medal was awarded to those territorial soldiers who were serving in their units before 4 August 1914 and who had given an undertaking, either verbally, or in writing, by 30 September 1914, to serve outside of the United Kingdom. Eligibility was determined by having served overseas between 4 August 1914 and midnight on 11 November 1918. Just 33,934 of these medals were awarded. A very low amount when one considers that the British War Medal, a more commonly issued

The Territorial Force War Medal (TFWM). (*Author's photo*)

Great War Campaign medal, was awarded to well over 6.5 million recipients.

Arthur's eligibility draws us to the question of his age and the fact that he could not legally have sailed with the battalion when they first embarked for France in March 1915. At that time, Arthur would only have been 18 – nearly a year too young for the minimum active service age of 19. Therefore, the only way he could have done this would have been to have lied about his age, as did many of his peers. However, to do this makes no real sense. Although his service record no longer exists, it seems a more likely scenario that he originally enlisted with his battalion as a boy soldier. This would also mean that a record existed of his true age and enlistment details, prior to the outbreak of war. Thus, this would prove his eligibility for the award, albeit posthumously.

Matters become clearer still when considering the fact that the Territorial Force War Medal was awarded only to those soldiers who had not been awarded either the 1914 or 1914-15 Star. Therefore, although there is no way now of knowing when Arthur was first sent to fight, we can say that he could not have arrived on the Western Front before at least 31 December 1915. Accordingly, no record exists of Arthur being awarded the 1914-15 Star under his original service number of 2083. It therefore seems safe to assume that Arthur was retained in the battalion reserve until such time as he was eligible for active service.

The only definite information we have about Arthur's service is that he enlisted at Leamington Spa. As with a significant number of his comrades, Arthur was killed on 8 October 1917 – the day after the battalion was relieved from the positions they had won and held during the Battle of Broodseinde.

After his death, his mother, Susan, received Arthur's savings of £5.9/2d and a war gratuity of £15.10/-. A dependant's pension of 5/- a week was awarded to Arthur's father, Walter.

Arthur's body was never recovered from the battlefield and he is therefore remembered on the memorial wall to the missing at Tyne Cot Cemetery. His name is also commemorated on the town war memorial erected in Euston Place, Leamington Spa.

Irvine Cooke – Sergeant (A Coy) 265430

Killed in action on 4 October 1917, aged 24 years.
Buried at Cement House Cemetery.
Grave reference: X. D. 19.

Headstone inscription:

I AM THE RESURRECTION AND THE LIFE

Irvine Cooke was born in the last quarter of 1892 in the Clifton Wood area of Bristol. Both his father, Alfred, and mother, Florence (nee Halliday), were tailors by profession. In the year immediately prior to Irvine's birth, the Cooke family, which also comprised Irvine's older brother, Stanley, and his aunt, Rose Halliday, who was also a tailoress, were living at 2, Belle Vue Crescent, Clifton. This was a three-storey Georgian terraced property in a part of town populated mostly by working-class professionals such as police constables, painters and nurses. Like many of the properties on that street, it is likely that it was divided into rooms, mostly to let for families.

Sadly, after only four years of marriage and at just 34 years of age, Alfred died. He was laid to rest in the parish of his birth, East Clevedon, on 27 June 1895. Unusually for the time, Irvine had not been christened by the time of Alfred's death. However, just a little over a month after Alfred's burial, Irvine, along with his elder brother Stanley and little sister Violet, born in 1894, were all christened at St Peters, Church of England parish church, Clifton Wood.

Inevitably, with Alfred's income gone, the family had to move to more modest accommodation. This was a stone-terraced house at 7, Southernhay Crescent, just a few streets away from their old home and close to the banks of the busy River Avon.

Nevertheless, the 1901 Census shows that Belle Vue Crescent was soon to be the family home once more. By then, Florence had moved her family back to the street, taking up occupancy at number three. Living with them too was

Florence's 25-year-old sister, Esther. Though, a closer look at both the 1891 and 1901 Census likely reveals the reason for Florence wanting to return to the street: her younger brother, Egbert Halliday, and his family were resident in the same building throughout those years. They would no doubt prove to be a major source of comfort and support for Florence as she worked to bring her family up as a widow.

No further civil records exist for Irvine, so we cannot say what trade he had taken up by the time he was of an age to work. Although his service record doesn't exist either, we do know that he enlisted at Newport, Monmouthshire as Private 1860 of the Monmouthshire Regiment (Monmouths). Again, due to the lack of records, we cannot say when he entered the Western Front theatre of war, or when he was transferred to the Royal Warwicks.

As a member of A Coy, Irvine was not involved in the first phase of the assault on the morning of 4 October 1917. Instead, his Company would follow up as part of a second assault group with B Coy. The troops followed in under cover of a protective creeping artillery barrage, with A Coy splitting off to attack the battalion's second objective, Terrier Farm, which they subsequently achieved. It is not known if Irvine was killed during this phase of the attack, or later in the day.

Although he now lies in Cement House Cemetery, this does not mean Irvine's body was removed from the battlefield at the time of the assault and given a burial. Certainly, Cement House Cemetery itself was begun in the previous August and was in use at the time by field ambulances and units of the line, alike. However, fierce fighting took place on the first day of this major offensive, followed by two days dug in to hold the positions won. Irvine's body, like other fallen men, could not be recovered for burial during this period, or afterwards. Instead, CWGC records reveal that Irvine lay where he fell until he was eventually exhumed during body recovery operations carried out during 1920. The recovery teams were able to identify him by a piece of identity disc found with the body and he was then taken with other men recovered from the field and re-buried at Cement House Cemetery.

There is, of course, no way to know how news of her son's body being found was received by Florence. By April 1918, she had moved to 13, Prince Street, Queens Square, Bristol. As Irvine's sole legatee, she had received his savings of £7.6/2d and a war gratuity of £17.00. She was also awarded a weekly pension of 5/-.One would like to think that she perhaps drew some comfort in knowing that her son had at least been laid properly to rest.

Cecil John Core – Private 34023

Missing presumed dead on 8 October 1917, aged 20 years.
Commemorated at Tyne Cot Memorial.
Panel 25.

At the time of Cecil's birth in Camberwell, Surrey on 3 June 1897, Charles Browne Core and his wife, May (nee Gooch), had already established a sizeable family in the well-to-do area of Dulwich Village in South London. Preceded by four sisters and two brothers, Cecil, or 'Jackie' as he was also known, would later become brother to a further four sisters. However, he would subsequently lose an older brother, Arthur, who died, aged just five, in 1900. Also, his younger brother, Norman, died soon after birth in 1905. This left Cecil with just one older brother, Charles Gooch Core. He was around twelve years Cecil's senior and was also known as 'Dickie'.

Portrait of Private Cecil Core.
(*Photo provided courtesy of Alleyn's School, Dulwich and used with kind permission of Nicola Waddington, Alleyn's School archivist*)

It is clear the family were comfortably off, with Cecil's father earning a good living as a builder and artist. Although, despite Charles Snr's repeated efforts spanning over forty years, he never succeeded in his goal of having one of his works exhibited at the Royal Academy Summer Exhibition. However, a good number of his works still exist today and testify to Charles's considerable talent as an artist.

Despite his disappointment, Charles was easily able to provide an extremely comfortable life for his family, with the 1901 and 1911 Census showing the family in residence at 1, Commerce Place, Dulwich Village. For Cecil, as with his siblings, this ensured that his childhood was also both stable and secure.

School life started at Dulwich Hamlet Junior School and then, in September 1910, on to the prestigious Alleyn's Grammar School, also in Dulwich. In July 1915, straight after leaving Alleyn's, Cecil joined the London and County Westminster Bank as a junior clerk.

It is not known when Cecil actually joined the army, only that he initially enlisted at Camberwell as Private 202196 of the East Kent Regiment (The

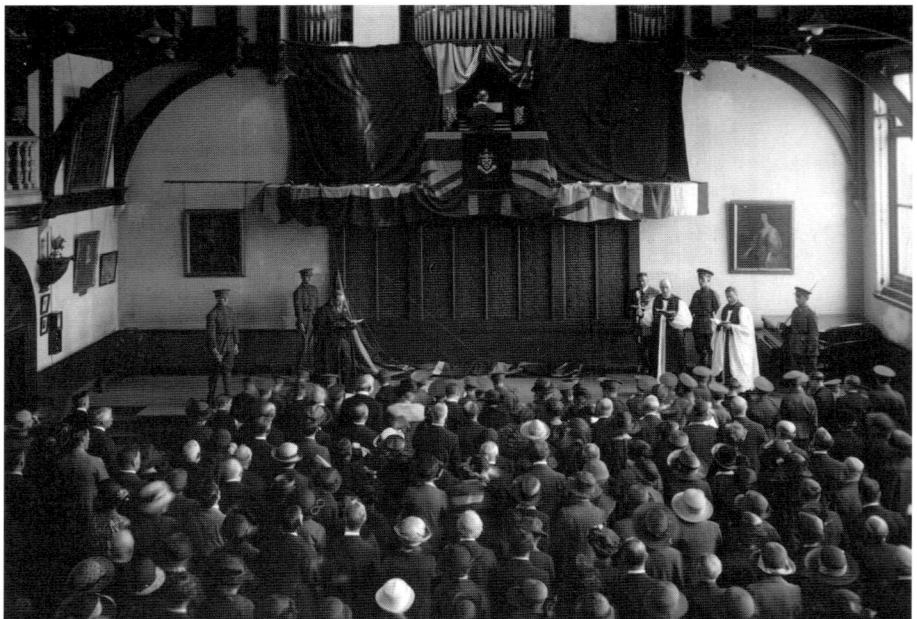

The unveiling, in 1922, of the organ commissioned to commemorate those Alleyn's old boys who fell in the Great War. (*Photo provided courtesy of Alleyn's School, Dulwich and used with kind permission of Nicola Waddington, Alleyn's School archivist*)

Buffs), sometime in the month after 9 September 1916. From there, he would eventually transfer to the 1/7 Royal Warwicks as Private 34023.

Also unknown to us is when his brother, Charles, enlisted. Though what we can say is that Charles subsequently received a commission and served as a 2nd Lieutenant in the 11 Bn Royal Fusiliers, City of London Regiment. The fact that Charles received a commission does beg the question as to why Cecil did not seek a commission too. After all, his background would have given him a major advantage, had he wished to become an officer. Though, the answer to that will probably never be known.

On 10 August 1917, Cecil was with his battalion in the St Julien sector, just outside of Ypres. At this time, his brother's battalion was involved in an advance along the Menin Road, when they came under heavy artillery fire. This caused the battalion to divert into Glencorse Wood, where they encountered heavily defended German positions and were met with a hail of small arms and machine-gun fire. Seventeen officers and 328 other ranks were killed or wounded as a result. Charles was one of the officers lost that day.

It is impossible to know how Cecil reacted to the news of his brother's death. He, like many other men on the front who had received such terrible news, simply had to carry on with their duties. Cecil did that, right up to the point that he lost his own life, just short of two months later, on 8 October.

No pension records could be located for Cecil, although we do know that his father was named as his sole legatee and received payment of his savings of £2.4/4d, along with a war gratuity of £3.10/-. As for Charles; his pension record states only that he left a widow, Amy, who would no doubt have been in receipt of his total effects of £21.7/-. No final pension amount is recorded on the card.

Because neither of the brothers' remains were recovered for burial, their names were subsequently added to memorials to the missing in the Ypres Sector. Charles's name is therefore inscribed on the Menin Gate, while Cecil's name was added to the Tyne Cot memorial wall. He was also remembered by his old school, Alleyn's, which commissioned a beautiful organ, incorporating wooden panelling inscribed with names of Alleyn's boys who lost their lives in service to their country. The organ was unveiled in 1922 and originally recorded the names of the 264 old boys who died in the Great War. A further 130 names were subsequently added to commemorate those lost in World War Two.

John James Croall – Captain

On attachment from 5th Bn, Royal Scots Fusiliers.
Killed in action on 4 October 1917, aged 24 years.
Commemorated at Tyne Cot Memorial.
Panel 60A.

Born in Edinburgh on 9 June 1892, John James Croall was the only son of John and Sarah Croall and the younger brother of his only sibling, Mary, who was three years his senior.

While the family were natives of Edinburgh, Scotland, the nature of John Snr's job as a travelling stationery salesman saw the family relocate at least twice as John's work took him south of the border and into England.

The 1901 Census records the family living at 130, City Road, Rotton Park, Birmingham. An area located broadly between Edgbaston and Ladywood. The house they rented was a spacious terraced house, large enough to require a domestic servant – one Esther Barley, originally from Bromsgrove and then only 15 years old.

By the time of the 1911 census, the family had relocated to Bristol, again having taken up occupancy in another comfortable, terraced house. This time at 45, Florence Park in the Redland area. However, it is clear that the move to

Bristol had taken place some years before the census, as young John had already won a junior city scholarship and had been studying at Bristol Grammar School since 1905. He had also become a keen member of the Robert Thorne Troop of the 56th Bristol Boys Scouts.

In 1912, John left Bristol Grammar School to become a clerk with the tobacco company W.D. & H.O. Wills. However, in September of 1914, by agreement with the War Office and the company executive, it was decided that the percentage of company employees who could be released for war service would be extended. John would be one of those additional employees released for service.

Initially, he would go on to join the 3/28 (County of London) Battalion of the London Regiment, also known as the Artists Rifles. However, this battalion was not formed until 1 January 1915, so it would not be until after this date that John initially became Private 3945 Croall.

John subsequently obtained a commission with the 5th Bn, Royal Scots Fusiliers and entered the Western Front theatre on 8 September 1916. He then joined the 1/7 Royal Warwicks on attachment as a lieutenant on the fourteenth of that month.

By 4 October 1917, John had been promoted to captain and was in command of C Coy, which, along with D Coy, was the first wave of the battalion into the attack that morning. Given the circumstances set out in the battalion war diary and the account set out in his commanding officer's letter to his parents, it appears that John was among the very first of the soldiers to die under a hail of German defensive fire. An excerpt from the letter explains how John came to fall:

> *He was a fine company-commander, and everyone loved him. The men would have followed him anywhere, and are very much cut up at his death. He died gallantly leading his company on the 4th October. A machine-gun opened fire on his company just as they started to advance, shooting him through the head and killing him instantly. I cannot express how deeply I feel for you. He is a great loss to us all.*

Of course, it is known that, in many letters sent back from the front, the authors of notes describing a death to a loved one commonly wrote that their death was swift and painless. The obvious intention was to spare the grieving relative from knowing what was often the more gruesome or brutal truth. At face value, such could have been the case here. However, the battalion war diary account mentioned above, cross-referenced with corporal Arthur Hutt's VC citation, supports the contents of the letter. Both attest to the fact that the opening attack was ravaged by heavy fire from machine guns. Also, a high number of officers and NCOs were either killed or injured in the opening minutes of the attack. We can perhaps therefore have faith in the writer's implication that John's death was mercifully quick as he became an early victim of the fire put down by the deadly efficient German machine guns.

Although John's pension record has not survived, existing army records show that he did leave savings of £26.16/11d and a war gratuity of £5.00 was also paid to his family. His probate information was published in December of 1917 and confirmed that he left his total estate of £331.14/5d to his mother, Sarah.

Along with many of his men, John's body was never recovered for burial. His name was therefore added to the memorial to the fallen at Tyne Cot. It was also added to the memorial screen for the fallen former pupils of Bristol Grammar School, which was formally unveiled on 5 October 1922. Also, after his father died in 1941 and was laid to rest at Springbank Cemetery, Aberdeen, Scotland, John's name was added in memoriam to the headstone.

William Joseph Crutchlow – Private 266116

Missing presumed killed in action on 8 October 1917, aged 30 years.
Commemorated at Tyne Cot Memorial.
Panel 25.

The first of five children born to Joseph Crutchlow, a market gardener, and his wife, Mary Jane (nee Tatlow), William Joseph Crutchlow was born in Coventry in July 1887. The first record of the young family appears in 1891, when they were living at 4 House, 2 Court in Conways Place, in central Coventry. This was accommodation comprising just four rooms and with them by this time was William's baby sister, Edith, who had been born in the March of 1890. Eventually, William and Edith would be joined by siblings: Nellie, born in 1894, followed by Ernest in 1897 and Frank in 1898.

By the time of the 1901 Census, the family had moved to similar, four-roomed accommodation, in the courts of York Street, located just outside of the city centre. In 1908, William married Ada Emily (nee Goode) in the second quarter of 1908. Their only child, Alice Maud, was then born in July of the same year. The 1911 Census subsequently records them all as living in three-room accommodation at 7 Court, 17 House, Spon Street, again located just on the edge of the city centre.

William's occupation is recorded on the census as a cycle finisher and by the time he had volunteered to enlist, he was then employed by Messrs Hobart and Bird, a Coventry-based manufacturer of motorcycles.

Enlistment for William was on 20 November 1914, at Coventry, when he initially became Private 3439 of the 2/7 Royal Warwicks. However, although William would undergo his basic training and remain in the battalion reserve, he would not immediately be sent to the front. Instead, on 16 September 1915, he was released by the army to engage in vital war work in order to service government contracts. The only real clue as to what this work might have been is held in his service record, which states only that he was lodged at 92, King Street in Loughborough. However, the record does not name the employer, therefore denying any further opportunity for investigation as to the possible nature of the work.

William returned to military duty on 17 July 1916 and from there he was subsequently sent to France on 9 September. On 17 October he joined the 1/7 Royal Warwicks at St Amand, where the battalion was engaged in an extended period of training.

Service life was clearly a hard experience for William. Even prior to his withdrawal from army service for war work, William had already fallen foul of army discipline. Initially, he had been reported for being absent without leave from Blackmore Camp for two days from 9 May 1915. A further unauthorised absence of one day while at Ludgershall Camp on 23 August 1915 earned William the loss of a day's pay with a further seven days confined to barracks.

Things did not improve for William in the field, either. He initially fell ill with bronchitis, probably in early March 1917 and was sent to the Corps Rest Station (CRS). However, his condition failed to improve and he was then transferred to the 1/2 North Midland Field Ambulance (NMFA). By 29 March his condition had deteriorated to the point that it was recorded as having a severe debility and he was admitted to the 10th General Hospital at Rouen, not returning to the battalion until 28 May. The day before the battalion relieved the 8th Worcesters in the line at Louverval.

William's struggle to cope with the strict routine of service life resurfaced on 3 August when he was late on parade, refused to produce his paybook when ordered to do so and was insolent to an NCO.

There is, of course, no way to know why William chose to act this way but the reaction was swift. The next day he was sentenced to the maximum term of 21 days' Field Punishment No.1. Essentially, this would mean that he would be tied to a static object such as a post, frame or cart wheel and left to stand there for up to two hours a day and for up to three days out of four.

However, it seems unlikely that William completed the full term of the punishment, given that the battalion moved up to the St Julien Sector on 11 August, where he is recorded as being wounded in the field. Curiously, there is a date range for the wounding of 10 to 15 August, rather than a single date.

However, his service record also records that he remained in the field. The date range may therefore indicate how long he had suffered from the effects of the wounding, which would, at any rate, have been relatively minor, given that he was not removed from duty.

As the fighting in the Ypres sector continued into the autumn, William remained with his unit. Ultimately, he would see out the action of 4 to 7 October, only to be posted as missing in action the following day. His widow, Ada, would ultimately receive a widow's pension of 26/8d per week, with an additional weekly sum of 10/- for their daughter, Maud.

William's body was never recovered from the battlefield and he is therefore remembered on the memorial wall at Tyne Cot. It is not known if he is commemorated locally.

Charles Cushings – Private 29302

Died on 8 October 1917, aged 19 years.
Commemorated at Tyne Cot Memorial.
Panel 25.

The oldest of three sons, Charles Cushings was born in Norwich on 15 May 1898, to Charles, a labourer, and his wife, Clara Lucy (nee Brewster).

In April 1900, Charles's first brother, Donald, was born and by 1901 the census records the family as living in four shared rooms at 4, Wright's Buildings, Norwich. Clara's step-sister, Florence Kendall, is recorded as the head of household and also resident is Clara's father, Samuel Brewster, an 81-year-old retired builder and by then, a widower. Although brother Donald is recorded on the census for 1901, records show that he died in the January, so likely very soon after the census record was completed.

As with the 1911 Census, Charles's father does not appear on the 1901 record. Certainly, as a man previously employed as a labourer, it could be assumed that he may have been working away from home. This would explain his absence within the family record. However, an interesting find in the 1911 Census more strongly suggests an alternative explanation.

In it, one Charles Cushings appears in the record as an attendant at the nearby Norwich lunatic asylum. Therefore, if we set aside his previous occupation, we have a male of the same age, born in Norwich in 1877 and in residential employment, close to his family. Given the rarity of the name itself in the records, it would therefore seem reasonable to suggest that this man is in fact Charles's father, giving a more clear and plausible explanation as to why he is not recorded as living with his family. Furthermore, the only

The Norwich Roll of Honour. (*Photo credit – Norfolk Museums Service, War Memorials Online*)

other explanation – that the couple may have separated – does not seem likely as later records relating to Charles junior's military service indicate they are still married.

With regard to the family details in the 1911 Census, it shows that the family had moved to five-room accommodation at 93, Belvoir Street, Dereham Road, Norwich. By this time Clara had given birth to another son, Arthur, born in 1909, and had moved in with her sister, Alice Waspe, her husband, William, and their two daughters, Mildred and Lorna. Clara was by then working locally as a boot sewer.

Nothing is known about any work Charles may have been engaged in prior to enlistment and it is only possible to say that he enlisted at Norwich, in the month after 9 September 1916. The location for Charles's enlistment would most certainly mean that he did not join the Royal Warwicks directly.

The next time he appears in the records is when he is initially recorded as missing in action on 8 October 1917. By the time Charles was presumed dead, his parents were living at 24, Barn Road and it is Clara who receives a dependant's pension of 3/6d a week. His father is named as the recipient of his son's savings of £3.12/3d and a war gratuity of £3.00.

Charles's name is recorded alongside those of his comrades at Tyne Cot who were never recovered from the battlefield. He is also remembered on the Norwich Roll of Honour. This records the names of the 3,544 men from the Norwich area who, like Charles, gave their lives for their country.

Benjamin Deakin – Private 2788

Died on 8 October 1917, aged 22 years.
Commemorated at Tyne Cot Memorial.
Panel 25A.

Located close to the market town of Atherstone, North Warwickshire and around fifteen miles from Coventry is the village of Baddesley Ensor. As with many of the local towns and villages in that part of the county, the village had long been involved in coal mining and it is here, in the second quarter of 1895, that Benjamin Deakin was born into a typical coal mining family.

The youngest son of George Deakin, a coal miner's hewer, and Ellen (nee Chetwynd), he was baptised at the parish church of St Nicholas's in 1897. The family itself was a very large one and from the 1901 Census, it can be seen that George and Ellen were blessed with no less than eight sons and three daughters.

By the time of the 1911 census, six of the children were still living with their parents and ranged in age from Charles, the eldest son, at 35 years old, to the youngest, Ellen, who was born after Benjamin in the January of 1898. The whole family lived in a cottage comprising just five rooms. With the exception of Charles, who was a bricklayer's labourer, and Ellen, who was only 13, they were all engaged in coal production. At just 15, Benjamin himself was employed in the local pit as a clipper, attaching the ropes that hauled the pit carts from the coal face to the lifts.

Though Benjamin's service record no longer exists, it is still possible to provide some detail regarding his enlistment and service. Initially, he enlisted at Nuneaton, probably in the August that war was declared. At the time, the Royal Warwicks were issuing consecutive four-figure service numbers. It is therefore possible, given the numerical value of the numbers issued in any one month, to calculate that Benjamin likely joined up somewhere in the period covering August and September 1914.

Benjamin was awarded the 1914-15 Star and his medal index card confirms that he initially joined the 1st Bn Royal Warwicks. This was a regular army battalion that had landed in France on 22 August 1914, as part of the BEF. He would ultimately join his unit, in France, on 8 December 1914.

While serving in France in June of the following year, Benjamin would learn that his mother, Ellen, had passed away, aged 62. His misfortunes then continued the following month when he was wounded and evacuated back to England on 11 July. Although casualty lists show him as being admitted to Chatham Hospital in Kent, it does not record the nature of his injury. Though, any injury requiring evacuation to England would normally be relatively serious, requiring convalescence and rehabilitation. The list also shows that by then, he had been promoted to lance corporal.

The stone memorial obelisk in the grounds of St Nicholas Parish Church, Baddesley Ensor. (*Photo credit – Nuneaton & North Warwickshire Family History Society and War Memorials Online*)

Benjamin would eventually become fit to return to combat duties and go on to also serve with 2nd Bn Royal Warwicks, 16th Bn (Reserve) Royal Warwicks and lastly, the 1/7 Royal Warwicks. Again, casualty lists also confirm that he was wounded at least once more, around August to September 1916. Though again, the available records do not show the nature of this wounding, when he was serving with the various battalions, or when and why he was demoted to private.

As has been already referenced, the fact that he was a regular soldier and had served in a number of battalions meant that he was never reallocated a new service number, as was the case with men in territorial units. The reason why he retained a four-figure service number at the time of his death therefore indicates that he was likely still in service with a regular unit when the TF was renumbered in early 1917.

Benjamin eventually became one of the many casualties suffered by the 1/7 Royal Warwicks on 8 October, when he was initially reported as missing in action. Clearly, his loss must have been a grievous one for his family. Though mercifully, it appears that of the eight Deakin boys, he was the only one lost in the war.

Benjamin left his effects of £4.6/11d to his youngest sister, Ellen, who was also paid a war gratuity of £18.00. A dependant's pension of 4/- a week was also awarded to his father, George.

As well as the inclusion of his name on the Tyne Cot memorial wall, he is also remembered on the village war memorial at Baddesley Ensor, located on the grounds of St Nicholas's, the church in which he was baptised.

Henry Dickenson – Private 267023

Died on 8 October 1917, aged 34 years.
Commemorated at Tyne Cot Memorial.
Panel 25A.

Though it is not entirely clear where, Henry Dickenson was born in 1883 in a part of the Cotswolds in rural Gloucestershire, close to its southern border with Wiltshire. There is some suggestion that he was actually born in Evesham, Worcestershire, though his available census information confirms that he was actually born in Gloucestershire. The uncertainty as to where arises due to the fact that a number of census records spanning 1891 to 1911 record different birth places. These mention the villages of Sherston, Saddlewood and Leighterton, all of which lie within a few miles of each other. No further clarity is gained from the index of births for the year as it merely records that he was born in the first quarter of 1883 in the district of Chipping Sodbury. This being the municipal area covering the aforementioned villages.

Also, some of the information held in relation to Henry by the CWGC is incorrect too. Their information puts him at 40 years old at the time of his death. However, the aforementioned census and birth records clearly confirm that he was actually 34 when he fell.

At the time of Henry's birth, his natural father, James Dickenson, was still married to his mother, Fanny (nee Iles). The 1881 Census, compiled two years before Henry's birth, records that the couple already had three girls and a boy, the eldest being John, who was seven. However, by the time of the 1891 Census, Fanny had remarried to James Mann, a farm labourer. Of the five children from her previous marriage, only Henry, then eight, and his two sisters, Annie, 12, and Sarah, 10, remained with their mother. The oldest siblings, John and Elizabeth, appear to have gone to live with their father. The first new addition to the family, their half-brother, Charles Mann, had been born four years previously. The second was Mary, who was two years old at the time of the census.

By the time of the 1901 Census, an 18-year-old Henry was living independantly, lodging in the village of Cam, near Dursley and earning a living as a milk hand on a dairy farm. However, by the time the 1911 Census came round, he was working as a waggoner. Henry had also returned to live with his mother and step-father in Huntingford, near the village of Charfield, Gloucestershire. By this time, he was the only other person recorded as living at the property.

Henry enlisted at Wotton-under-Edge, a small market town in the area where he grew up. However, given the fact that his service record no longer exists, almost nothing else is known about his military service. His medal records show that he was only awarded the Victory Medal and the British War Medal and not a 1914-15 Star. Consequently, it is unlikely that he enlisted no earlier than late 1915. This is because any recipients of the 1914-15 Star

Wotton-under-Edge war memorial (*Photo credit – Ian S (Geograph), 2013, War Memorials Online*)

would have to have served in a theatre of war before 31 December 1915. That said, he could have enlisted earlier and been held on home duties or reserve, or unfit for combat for whatever reason, which delayed his entry into the fighting.

The fact that Henry has a six-figure service number means that he would have been serving in a TF unit when the men serving in those units were renumbered from March 1917 onwards. However, the number he received tells us only that he was part of the 1/7 Royal Warwicks when this took place, as he received a number from within the batch allocated to that particular battalion.

Ultimately, Henry was one of a number of soldiers reported as missing in action on 8 October 1917 and subsequently declared dead. His mother, Fanny, as his sole beneficiary, received his savings of £2.16/-, a war gratuity of £6.00 and a weekly dependant's pension of 5/-. At the time, Fanny was living at Huntingford Mill in Charfield. At some stage, she also became the licensee of the Old Plough pub, also in Charfield.

As well as the inclusion of his name on the memorial wall at Tyne Cot, Henry is commemorated on the village war memorial at Wotton-under-Edge, the place where he enlisted. The memorial contains the names of a further 114 men from the area, who also lost their lives in the Great War.

Thomas William Dunn – Private 265603

Died of wounds on 5 October 1917, aged 26 years.
Commemorated at Tyne Cot Memorial.
Panel 25A.

Thomas Dunn was born in January 1891 in South Shields, a small town lying on the mouth of the River Tyne, close to the city of Newcastle. At the time of Thomas's birth, the town was part of County Durham and sat at the heart of thriving ship building and coal mining industries.

The 1901 Census records that Thomas was the oldest son of 38-year-old Thomas Snr, a corporation labourer, and his wife, Jane. Also listed is Thomas's younger brother, Robert, who was two years old at the time of that census. Home was 26, Laygate Place, situated just a stone's throw from the Tyne itself. However, the area itself has long since been redeveloped and although some of the original street layout remains, the old houses have long gone.

By 1911, the family had relocated to 55, Brooklyn Road, Coventry. Close to the Bishopsgate Green and Foleshill areas of the city. By then, both Thomas and Thomas Snr were working as spinners. However, a distinction made within the census form gives a conclusive indication as to where Thomas Snr may have been working as it also notes that he is employed at an 'artificial silk works'. This can only be the Courtaulds factory, which was located just a few yards round the corner from the family home. Courtaulds had established a vast factory centred on the Foleshill Road in 1905 and it was then the only major manufacturer in Coventry engaged in the production of artificial silks, or rayon, as it is otherwise known.

Interestingly, though no direct clue exists as to where young Thomas was employed, the census form does make the distinction that he is working as a 'silk spinner'. Also, unlike his father's entry, it does not say that he works with artificial silk. It is therefore possible that he was actually engaged by another local firm, Cash's. Again, located just around the corner from the family home, Cash's mill turned out such things as silk ribbons and silk name tapes.

As with the modest end-of-terrace family home in Brooklyn Road, substantial parts of both the Courtaulds and Cash's works still exist today, albeit they have both since been repurposed and exist mainly as office space and apartments.

Thomas's service record has not survived and it is therefore not possible to say exactly when he enlisted, although we do know that this was in Coventry and probably around October 1914. Given that no record exists of him receiving a 1914-15 Star, it is clear that he did not arrive on the Western Front before at least the end of 1915 and may therefore have been retained in battalion reserves.

It is interesting to note at this point that Thomas died at the age of 26. This therefore begs the question as to why he had not enlisted prior to this date. After all, given his eligibility for service from the outset of war, he may well have attracted some very unwelcome attention from those members of the public who would have pointed out that, at his age, he should be in uniform.

A possible explanation for this is that he was actually retained in his civilian profession for the benefit of the war effort. As a skilled silk spinner, his services would have been needed to maintain production of such an important commodity. In support of this theory is the fact that none other than his battalion comrade, Corporal Arthur

A Home Service Badge, issued in 1915. (*Author's photo*)

Hutt VC, had been temporarily withdrawn from service to continue his work at the Courtaulds factory. However, as with men in many other reserved trades or occupations, more and more of them were released for service, as the need for fighting men increased. Hence the possibility that, as with Arthur Hutt being returned to service, Thomas was also eventually released for enlistment.

As suggested above, men of fighting age who were seen on the streets without uniforms could find themselves subjected to some very direct and public criticism from people on the street, mainly women and young girls, for not enlisting. A very plain but scathing indication could often be made, with the man being publicly issued with a white feather, which denoted cowardice. Therefore, in order to avoid this, the government arranged for the issue of Home Service lapel badges, to be issued each year. These would, in theory at least, allow men on war work to go about their daily business, unmolested.

Thomas died from wounds on 5 October 1917, when he and his comrades were defending the gains of the previous day. His body was never recovered for burial, which suggests he was never evacuated from the forward areas and most likely died either on or not far from the front line. Had he been evacuated to a CCS or one of the Field or General Hospitals, it is more likely he would have been buried in an established cemetery with his whereabouts being properly recorded and his grave surviving the war.

It is therefore more probable that he was treated for his wounds either at, or very close to the front by battlefield medics, or at a Forward Aid Post or Dressing Station. Depending on where he died, his body was then either left on the battlefield, or buried close to the front, where the grave was either subsequently lost or destroyed.

Thomas left savings of £13.12/1d to his mother, Jane, who also received a war gratuity of £14.00. But, although Jane is recorded as Thomas's dependant on the relevant pension record, it does not record that she was ever awarded an amount, or when any payment was made.

Thomas is commemorated at the Tyne Cot memorial to the missing. However, other than inclusion in Coventry's Roll of Honour, it is not known whether he is included on any of the city's local war memorials.

Joseph Earl – Private 20522

Died on 8 October 1917, aged 19 years.
Commemorated at Tyne Cot Memorial.
Panel 25A.

Born in the Bordesley area of Birmingham in July 1898, Joseph Earl was baptised on 7 August, in the Parish of St Basil's, Deritend. He was the fourth child of a coal carter, Thomas, and his wife, Caroline (nee Sheppard).

Joseph was born into a rapidly growing family and by the time of the 1901 Census, he had gained another brother, George, who was then seven months old. Home was 126, Glover Street in Small Heath, Birmingham. The area adjoins Bordesley and was a mixture of working-class dwellings and industrial buildings, chiefly concerned with manufacturing metal goods. Along with his parents, baby brother and 16-year-old sister, Mary Ann, Joseph shared his home with older brothers James, 11, Albert, nine, and William, seven. To add to the already cramped living conditions, Joseph's 62-year-old grandmother, Suzannah, was also living with the family, along with their cousins, Arthur Mouser, 19, and his sisters, 17-year-old Elizabeth and 10-year-old Hannah.

By the time of the 1911 Census, the family had moved just a short distance from their old home to 8, Kingston Road, also in Small Heath. This was a more spacious, eight-room property. By this time, although grandmother Suzannah was still living with the family, the three cousins had moved out and their place had been taken by three new siblings: Dora, eight, Frederick, five, and Robert, who was three. Joseph's older sister, Mary Ann, had also moved out by that time, but two of his older brothers were still living at home. James, then 21, was working as a brass dresser and 17-year-old William was a cabinet maker.

Albert, however, is not included in the census information for the address. Instead, he is shown as having joined the regular army and at the time of the census, he is recorded as Private 1757 Earl of the 2nd Bn Royal Warwicks, stationed at Whittington Barracks, near Lichfield, Staffordshire.

At the outbreak of war, the family were still resident in Small Heath. Though, by this time, they had moved to 107, Greenway Street. The first of the brothers to enlist were William and James. William was 20 years old at the time and working as a carter. His service record still survives and shows that he enlisted as Gunner 55678 for service with the Royal Garrison Artillery (RGA) at No.3 Recruiting Office, Suffolk Street, Birmingham on 1 December 1914. He was then posted to the 16th Siege Battery, which, as with all of the RGA batteries, operated large calibre artillery pieces. He remained with that unit for the duration of his service.

James's service record does not exist but we do know he enlisted at Birmingham around April 1915. He was around 24 years of age. Rifleman A/1610 James Earl initially served with the 8th Bn of the King's Royal Rifle Corps (KRRC), but would go on to serve in France with the 9th KRRC, later achieving promotion to lance corporal.

No service record exists for Joseph either, so it is therefore difficult to shed much light on his service. However, information held on army medal rolls, war gratuity payments and the official summaries of those soldiers killed during the Great War have allowed for the provision of some detail. It is therefore likely that Joseph also enlisted in Birmingham. He was then accepted for service around March 1916, just a few months before his eighteenth birthday, becoming Private 20522 of the 16th (Reserve) Bn Royal Warwicks.

Joseph would likely still have been in reserve when he learned of the death of his eldest brother, James, who was killed in action on 15 September 1916. James fell when his unit took part in an attack on Delville Wood, a part of the Somme campaign.

In a further tragedy for his family, Joseph, having joined his unit on the Western Front, would fall just under thirteen months later, on 8 October 1917. However, the Earl family would suffer yet more grief just over a month later, when William was also killed in action on 9 November 1917, just outside Ypres.

Neither Joseph's nor James's bodies were subsequently recovered from the battlefield and their names are therefore remembered alongside other missing comrades at separate locations on the Western Front. James is remembered at the Thiepval Memorial and Joseph's name is inscribed on the memorial wall at Tyne Cot.

William's body was recovered from the battlefield, however, and he rests at Canada Farm Cemetery, located just to the northwest of Ypres and just a short distance away from where his younger brother, Joseph, fell. He lies buried in Plot 3, Row F, Grave 20. The following inscription was added to his headstone at the request of his father, Thomas:

SAFE IN PORT. PEACE AFTER STORM.

After his death, William's personal effects were recovered and his family notified.

On New Year's Day of 1918, his mother, Caroline, wrote a letter to the War Office to say that she had not yet received her son's belongings and asked for them to be forwarded. Of the three sons she had lost, the only things that could help her feel any closer to one of them now were William's identity disc, some letters and photos, two pocket cases, a religious book, a leather belt, a pair of scissors and a pocket knife. Also recovered were a cigarette case with vesta case and lighter, a metal pencil case and two leather purses containing four coins.

The grief that the Earl family must have felt at losing three boys must have been immense. It is evident in the fact that their mother wanted so much to take possession of a handful of humble but deeply personal belongings. As well as those few items, the family subsequently received war gratuities for all three sons and also payment of their savings. James left savings of £2.16/8d and a war gratuity of £8.10/-. William left £5.18/7d and a gratuity of £14.00. Joseph left savings of £7.2/11d and a gratuity of 6.10/-.

Thomas and Caroline Earl clearly suffered much from the loss of three sons. They must also have been beside themselves with worry too after their deaths. Not only was their oldest surviving son, Albert, still serving on the Western Front, but their second youngest son, George, later enlisted for service with the Royal Air Force on 26 September 1918 as Airman 298396 Earl. He was 18 years old at the time of enlistment and as such, never got to see action before the end of the war. He returned to Birmingham after the war and became a goods checker on the railways.

Albert, who started his service some years before war broke out, served throughout the conflict. He was a member of the BEF, receiving the 1914 Star. Records show that he later transferred to the Machine Gun Corps (MGC) and rose to the rank of warrant officer class II (sergeant major). He subsequently transferred back to the 2nd Royal Warwicks upon commission and survived the war, ending his service with the rank of captain.

The story of the Earl family is not only one of immense sacrifice, but also an example of the unquestioning service given by so many in their nation's time of need. As a final note to their story, it is understood that the three fallen Earl brothers were included on a memorial plaque erected on Greenway Street, commemorating the men of the street who also fell in the Great War. However, the memorial itself has long since disappeared as the area has undergone extensive redevelopment over the years.

Albert Eldridge – Private 300023

Died 4 October 1917, aged 36.
Commemorated at Tyne Cot Memorial.
Panel 25A.

Albert Ernest Eldridge was born in Langton, Kent in April 1881. At the time of his birth his family were living close to the town of Tonbridge in Kent and his father, William Edward Eldridge, was the patron of Coffee Shop No.3, the Waterman's Club, in Prospect Place, which he ran with his wife, Eleanor (nee Lewis).

By the time of Albert's birth, the couple already had three other children; Philadelphia, four, three-year-old William and one-year-old Eleanor. However, the 1891 Census records that the family had then moved to 199, Upper Fant Road, Maidstone, Kent as the boarders of Charles and Emily Clarke. By this time, the couple had further expanded their family with twins, Percy and Charles. Another daughter, Emily, and two sons, Ernest and John, had also arrived by then. Conditions must therefore have been very cramped in their small, terraced house, a building that still exists today.

Albert's father, William, is not listed as resident at this address. Though interestingly, his mother, Eleanor, is not recorded as working. It is therefore possible that William was working elsewhere and sending money home for his family's upkeep, hence Eleanor having no need to work and concentrating instead on bringing up the children. However, it has not been possible to verify this so far, as William has not yet been located on the census records for the year.

By 1901, the family had moved again and were living at 149, Milton Street, Maidstone. With five rooms or less to share, the Eldridge family would still have been struggling for space, particularly as Eleanor had given birth to two more daughters: Mabel and Kathleen. Though, sadly, one of their twin boys, Charles, had died in 1895, at just ten years old.

William was again living with his family by this time and working as a packer in a paper bag factory. By then 19 years old, Albert was also working for a living and is listed on the census as a journeyman bread baker. Yet, by the time of the 1911 Census, Albert had not only moved out of the family home but had also dispensed with his previous profession. The record confirms that he was still in Maidstone, but now working as a live-in boot boy at the 14-room Bull Hotel, 9, Gabriel's Hill, under the employ of 51-year-old licensed victualler, Mr William Russell. Resident also at the address is Mr Russell's wife, Eliza, and two live-in barmaids, Kate Fry and Laura Bowker. Today, the building that was formerly The Bull still exists, although it has since been converted to dwellings.

The year after the 1911 Census, Albert's father, William, passed away in October, at the age of 58. Albert's mother, Eleanor, also died, three years after her husband, in October 1915. She was 60 years old.

Albert's service record does not exist, but we do know that he enlisted at Maidstone around July 1916 and initially served as Private 6480 Eldridge of the Royal West Kent Regiment (Royal West Kents). At some point he transferred to the Norfolks and went through the TF renumbering process while with the 4th Battalion, having been issued with the new service number 201739. While we do not know when he transferred from the Royal West Kents to the Norfolks, the fact he was renumbered means that Albert would still have been with the Norfolks by 1 March 1917, when the renumbering process first started. Between then and his death Albert then transferred to 1/7 Royal Warwicks where he again received a new service number, 300023. This being the one he was allocated when he fell during the opening assault on German positions on 4 October 1917.

After Albert died, he left his savings to his siblings: John, Eleanor, Daisy, Kathleen, Percy, Mabel and lastly Ernest, who was serving in Bangalore, India with the 1st Reserve Bn the Oxfordshire and Buckinghamshire Regiment (Ox & Bucks). All received an equal share of Albert's savings of around 9/- each. However, his sister Kathleen also received a war gratuity of £6.10/-.

As his body was never recovered for burial, Albert's name is remembered on the memorial wall at Tyne Cot Cemetery. He is also commemorated locally on the Maidstone Borough War Memorial.

Robert William Etteridge – Private 300025

Died 4 October 1917, aged 20 years.
Commemorated at Tyne Cot Memorial.
Panel 25.

Born in Norfolk and christened in the parish of Attleborough on 4 April 1897, Robert William Etteridge was the fourth child of Robert James Etteridge, a farm labourer, and his wife, Appolonia (nee Pilgrim-Barnard), who, before their marriage, was a domestic servant. The couple married on 26 October 1884 and their first child, Frank, was born in 1887. Daughters Dolly and Eliza followed in 1889 and 1894 respectively. Their last child, Alfred, was born in 1900.

Previously resident in Connaught Road, Attleborough, by the 1901 Census, the family were living in the Garden House, White Horse Lane, also in Attleborough. This would remain the family home until at least 1937, when Robert's father passed away.

By the 1911 Census, Frank, Dolly and Eliza had left the family home and just Robert and Alfred remained. Robert was 14 by then and earning his keep as a butcher's errand boy.

Given the ages of all the Etteridge boys, it is possible that Frank and Alfred may also have signed up to fight. However, no conclusive record matches have so far been found in relation to their possible service. Although, it is known that both brothers survived the war, with Frank passing away in 1953 and Alfred in 1978.

Attleborough War Memorial. (*Photo credit – David Larkin, 2015, War Memorials Online*)

Because Robert's service record no longer exists, very little is known about his military service and the only firm information we have is that he initially enlisted at Norwich on 14 September 1914, joining a territorial unit, the 4th Bn the Norfolks, as Private 2700 Etteridge. At that time, he was only 17 years old.

As with the majority of territorial units, the 4th Bn The Norfolks comprised additional units. In this case, the 1/4 was augmented by the 2/4, which was a second line battalion, and the 3/4 reserve battalion. Although it is not known which of these units Robert served with, it is possible that the army discovered his true age at some stage and kept him at home with the reserves for a time. This being due to the fact that he would not have been eligible to serve overseas until his nineteenth birthday. However, it does mean that he could not have served with the 1/4 Norfolks as they sailed from Liverpool in July 1915, bound for Gallipoli. After being withdrawn from Gallipoli in December 1915, they then sailed for Alexandria and remained in Egypt and Palestine for the rest of the war.

It is not known when Robert transferred to the 1/7 Royal Warwicks. However, his final service number, as with his comrade Albert Eldridge, does indicate that he was with the battalion at least by 1 March 1917. This is because he received a new service number within the numerical sequence allocated to that unit.

Robert fell on 4 October 1917, which indicates that he fell either during the opening assault on the battalion's objectives for the attack, or in defence of the objectives achieved that day. His body was never recovered for burial.

After his death, Robert's father received his son's savings of £5.9/12d and a war gratuity of £13.10/-. On 26 February 1920, Robert's mother, Appolonia, received the first payment of her dependant's pension of 5/- a week. This was paid up until her death in 1927, after which, payment then transferred to Robert's father.

As Robert Etteridge has no known grave, his name is remembered at Tyne Cot memorial to the missing. His name is also inscribed locally on the Attleborough War Memorial Cross, which was unveiled in 1920 and stands at the junction of Queens Road and Exchange Street.

Sidney Albert Frost – Private 34026

Killed in action on 4 October 1917, aged 19.
Commemorated at Tyne Cot Memorial.
Panel 25.

Sidney Albert Frost is, unfortunately, a soldier about whom very little is known. Born in St Pancras, Middlesex in October 1897, Sidney was the fifth surviving child of Charles, a horse keeper, which is an alternative title for a groom, and Frances (nee Collins). Surviving documentation for Sidney is quite scant with just a handful of civil records, mostly made up of census information. Additionally, his service record no longer survives and therefore the story of his time in the army can only be told from a few surviving items relating to things such as pensions, effects and medal records.

He is first recorded in the 1901 Census and along with his parents, he lived with brothers Charles, 14, Frank, 9, and sisters Kate, 15, and Ada, 12. The family home at that time was in Cubitt Street, St Pancras, London.

By the time of the 1911 census, the family had moved just a short distance away to 7, Baker Street in Clerkenwell, London, WC1. At just 13 years old at the time, Sidney is recorded as attending school and has also acquired a younger brother in the years between censuses, namely six-year-old Ernest. However, because no further records have been recovered from the period between the census and his joining the army, it is not possible to say what work or trade he took on.

With regard to his enlistment, Sidney joined up at Holborn, London around September 1916. He initially signed up for service with a Territorial Force unit, the 2/4 Bn The Buffs. He was issued with the service number 202118. Because that number is part of the batch allocated to that unit, it therefore confirms that Sidney was still with The Buffs at the time of Territorial Force units being renumbered from March 1917 onwards. However, it is not possible to say when he transferred to the 1/7 Royal Warwicks. Consequently, the only thing we can say with certainty about his time with the unit is that he took part in the attack on Terrier Farm on 4 October and was killed during the fighting on that day.

Sidney had accumulated savings of £2.8/1d, which he left to his father, Charles, who also received a war gratuity of £3.10/-. However, it was his mother, Frances, who he nominated to receive a dependant's pension of 6/- a week.

As Sidney's body was never recovered from the battlefield, he is commemorated at Tyne Cot memorial to the missing. It is not known at this time whether he is commemorated on any memorials local to his home.

William Gardner – Private 265317

Died of wounds on 25 October 1917, aged 25.
Buried at St Sever Cemetery Extension, Rouen.
Grave ref: PIII.Q.11A.

Despite some effort to discover the facts behind William Gardner's life, he is, for now at least, another soldier about whom little is known. Confusingly, it appears that William has appeared in military records as not only Gardner, but also as Garner. This therefore creates the possibility that he is also recorded elsewhere as Gardiner or Gardener.

With regard to his early years, it is known that he was born in Leamington Spa, Warwickshire in 1892. He was the youngest of three sons born to Henry Gardner, the owner of a furniture shop, and Louisa (nee Berry), a seamstress. The 1901 Census records William, living with his parents and older brothers, Matthew, 12, and Phillip, 11, at 38 Clarendon Street, Leamington Spa. This was a modest but comfortable mid-terraced house, which still stands today.

Curiously, William was not baptised until 4 December 1898, when he would have been six years old. Further examination of the baptismal register reveals that not only was his brother Phillip baptised that same day, his oldest brother Matthew, then ten years old, was baptised just the previous month, on 30 November. All three baptisms carry the annotation 'adult' next to their respective entries. This presumably being because all three boys were by then too old for an infant baptism.

By the time of the 1911 Census, the Gardner family had moved just one road across town, to 5, Kenilworth Street. However, by this time both Matthew and William are not included as resident at the address and no trace of William has so far been found within the census returns for that year – at least not in Leamington Spa.

If the details of William's life prior to joining up are scarce, then the details of his army service are equally as sketchy. It is only really possible to say that he may have enlisted as early as around the outbreak of war – in or just before August 1914. Even this has only been loosely established by applying a back calculation involving the war gratuity that was paid upon his death. However, another discovery in the roll that records medal awards carries the service number 2071, which has then been typed over. William's current service number has then been added. This would loosely fit with the number sequence being issued to the 1/7 Royal Warwicks around the middle of 1914. However, some caution needs to be exercised in this regard as there is no record of William being issued with a 1914-15 Star, which, as one may expect, would confirm his entry into a theatre of war prior to 31 December 1915. Equally, the four-figure number could have just been a typographic error that has then been corrected by being struck out and the correct number entered.

Though it is not possible to know the circumstances that ultimately led to William dying of wounds, it is clear he was evacuated from the battlefield for treatment in Rouen. A number of General Hospitals had been established in the city for the reception and treatment of battlefield casualties. However, because the cemetery where William now lies received the dead from a large number of hospitals, it is not possible to identify the actual hospital where he was treated from the cemetery location alone.

When William died, he was the last of the battalion's soldiers to die on the Western Front, as they subsequently moved to Italy, along with the rest of the 143rd Division. His mother, Louisa, received his savings of £6.14/5d, along with a war gratuity of £14.10/-. Pension records also confirm Louisa as William's pension recipient, although no record of any amount awarded or payment being made is shown on the card.

The final mystery relating to William is whether or not he was commemorated on any war memorials in his home town. The only evidence that he may have been is a name, 'Pte W. T. Garner', inscribed on the town's main war memorial in Euston Place. However, due to the incorrect spelling of his surname, the presence of a previously unrecorded middle initial and the absence of any unit details, there is no way to say with any certainty that this name actually relates to William.

George Gilchrist – Private 268270

Died on 4 October 1917, aged 21.
Commemorated at Tyne Cot Memorial.
Panel 26A.

George Gilchrist was born in Kilmarnock, in the county of Ayrshire, Scotland on 8 September 1896. The son of George Snr, a coach trimmer, and Thomson (nee Morrison), he was the younger brother of David, who was around nine years older. He also had two sisters: Jeannie, two years his junior, and Jessie, who was six years younger. By faith, the family were Scottish Presbyterians and the family home was 29, West Netherton Street, in Kilmarnock. Though his service record does survive, few civil records exist to assist in telling the story of George's early years. However, we do know that in 1912, at the age of 15, he became an apprentice at the Kilmarnock branch of the National Bank of Scotland. We also know that, in March 1915, George became a clerk at the same branch and in October of the same year, he transferred to the bank's Glasgow office.

On 29 November 1915, while still working at the bank, George enlisted for service at the army recruiting office at 39, Bath Street, Glasgow and was initially placed on the reserve list. The record of his subsequent medical examination on 30 December that year describes him as 19 years and 3 months old, 5′ 5″ tall, around 108lbs and with a 35-inch chest. He was also of good physical development.

George was subsequently mobilised on 8 January 1916 and joined his unit as Private 5386 Gilchrist the following day. This was a local territorial battalion, the 1/9 (Glasgow Highland Battalion) of the Highland Light Infantry Regiment (Highland Light Infantry).

George would remain in the UK for much of 1916. However, his time with the Highland Light Infantry would be short and on 22 March he was transferred to the Royal Engineers (RE) Signals Company. George initially carried out driving duties and on 22 August he was transferred to Haynes Park in Bedfordshire for a course of instruction in the same.

By 27 November, George was transferred again, this time to training reserve. Though, by Christmas Eve, he was ready for active service and was transferred once more. This time to the 11th Bn Royal Warwicks, where he was issued with his new service number of 20527. George embarked at Southampton for Rouen the same day and by 13 January 1917, he transferred again – this time to the 1/7 Royal Warwicks, which were by then based at Warloy and already halfway through a month of intensive combat training.

George was subsequently issued with his final service number of 268270 and remained in the field with his battalion until 4 October, when he was killed in action during the attack centred on Terrier Farm. His body was never recovered from the battlefield.

After his death, his father, George, received his son's savings of £9.11/5d, along with a war gratuity of £7.10/-. George nominated his mother, Thomson, to receive a dependant's pension of 4/- a week, which was subsequently paid to his father when Thomson later passed away.

As well as his inclusion on the memorial wall at Tyne Cot, George is commemorated on the Scottish National War Memorial. He is further commemorated on a plaque dedicated to fallen employees of the National Bank of Scotland, which was initially erected at the bank's head office at St Andrew Square, Edinburgh. That plaque has since been relocated and is now at the Royal Bank of Scotland's Headquarters in Gogarburn, Edinburgh, though not on public display.

Douglas Walter Harris – Private 34049

Died of wounds on 8 October 1917, aged 21.
Buried at Poelcapelle British Cemetery.
Grave reference: LI. E. 2.

Douglas Harris was born in Camberwell, South London in October 1896. He was the second son of William Harris, a newspaper clerk, and his wife, Annie (nee Jarvis). The couple married at the parish church of St Anthony's, Nunhead in Camberwell on Christmas Day, 1893. By the time of the 1901 Census, they had made their home at 125, St George's Road, Camberwell and had started a family. Douglas was by then four years old with an older brother, six-year-old William, and a younger sister, Beatrice, aged two.

By the time of the 1911 Census, the family were still living at the same address, though by then they had been joined by another three children. These were nine-year-old Gladys, Frank, who was seven, and Colin, who was just two years old. Douglas was 14 by that time and working as a shop boy for a hairdresser. Though, the absence of one name from the census, Beatrice, did prompt some further investigation. As it transpired, Beatrice was listed as a patient at St Peter's Orphan and Convalescent Home for Girls, at Broadstairs in Kent. This home was originally established in 1866 and preferred to take in girls from London and the Diocese of Canterbury. However, although Beatrice is listed as a patient at the home, the reason is not known.

Because Douglas's service record does not exist, there is little that can be said with certainty about his time in the army. What is known is that he originally enlisted with the 2/4 The Buffs, probably sometime after October 1916. However, the service number issued to Douglas for this regiment is 202205, which indicates that he was still with that unit, at least around the time that territorial units were renumbered from March 1917 onwards. The 2/4 The Buffs was a second line unit and remained in England throughout the war. it is therefore likely that Douglas was transferred directly to the Royal Warwicks on completion of his training and deployment to the Western Front.

Though it cannot be said for certain on what date Douglas received the wounds that claimed his life, it is unlikely that they were sustained much earlier than the date of his death. The reason for this is that had he been wounded some days before, it is likely he would have already been evacuated from the immediate area of the battlefield and then laid to rest in one of the cemeteries serving the hospital, CCS or aid post he was treated at before he died. Instead, it appears from the available records that his remains were recovered from within a group of graves on or very close to the battlefield –

possibly casualties treated by battlefield medics, or at a forward aid post. The grave was marked with a plain cross and the post-war body recovery teams identified Douglas from an identity disc he was carrying. This bore the service number 202205 and he was originally misidentified as a soldier from The Buffs, but later correctly identified as a soldier of the Royal Warwicks. After recovery, his body was moved a short distance to Poelcapelle British Cemetery, which overlooks the battlefield where the assault on Terrier Farm took place.

After Douglas's death, his father, William, received his effects of £2.15/4d and a war gratuity of £3.00. As the nominated recipient of a dependant's pension, Douglas's mother, Annie, received a weekly pension of 6/- a week.

It is as yet unknown whether Douglas is commemorated on any war memorials close to his home.

Walter Hawkes – Private 300115

Killed in action on 8 October 1917, aged 19.
Commemorated at Tyne Cot Memorial.
Panel 26.

Walter Hawkes was born in Birmingham on 28 June 1898 and was the youngest child of Thomas and Elizabeth (nee Ingram). Thomas, a bedstead fitter, married Elizabeth at St Jude's parish church in Birmingham on 3 September 1882. By the time of Walter's birth, the couple already had five children: Elizabeth, Gertrude, George, Thomas and Edith. Home to the family at that time was 11, St James's Place, in the Aston area of the city.

The 1901 Census does not reflect any changes in the family dynamic, with all still being resident at the house in St James's Place and Thomas still being the sole breadwinner. However, by the 1911 Census, the Hawkes family's fortunes had much improved. By then, the entire family had moved into a larger house at 43, Hams Road in the Saltley area of Birmingham, a property that still exists today. A marked increase in the family income meant that Thomas Snr was no longer the sole earner in the house and they were able to aspire to something better. By this time, with the exception of Walter who was still at school, all of the Hawkes children were working. Elizabeth and Gertrude were employed as weavers at a mattress factory, while Edith was a switch hand at an incandescent light factory. Thomas was a fitter at a car factory and George was a hammer operator at a stamping works. It is therefore clear that, while they were very much a working-class family, they were now enjoying a much-improved standard of living, for which they had all worked hard to achieve.

There are no records to tell us what work Walter was engaged in prior to the war and the exact details of his enlistment are not known. It is known, though, that he enlisted at Birmingham and that this was not likely to have been before September of 1916. Initially, he was Private 7721 of the Norfolks, though at some unknown date he has then transferred to the Royal Warwicks. Nothing more is known of his service, save for the date of his death, when he was recorded as missing in action on 8 October 1917 and later presumed dead.

It was his father, Thomas, who received payment of a war gratuity of £3.00 upon Walter's death and his mother, Elizabeth, who subsequently received a weekly dependant's pension of 5/-.

As well as the inclusion of his name on the memorial to the missing at Tyne Cot, Walter is also remembered on the stone plaque erected in St James's Church in the village of Badsey, Worcestershire. Why Walter's name is recorded here is so far unknown as he has no known connection with the village. Indeed, the only possible connection to the area is via his father, Thomas. He is usually recorded as being born in Birmingham, but in the 1901 Census, he is shown as being born in 'Honeyport', Worcestershire. Nevertheless, this seems to be an unlikely reason for why a Worcestershire community would record his son as being one of their fallen, and so the mystery as to his inclusion remains.

George Hinde-Hayes MC – Company Sergeant Major 265385

Died of wounds on 10 October 1917, aged 34.
Buried at Wimereux Communal Cemetery.
Grave reference: VI. C. 21.

Inscription reads:

WAITING FOR THE DAWN TO BE
REUNITED HIS DUTY DONE R.I.P.

In the countryside between Rugby and Coventry lies the ancient Warwickshire village of Brinklow. It was there, on 8 July 1884, that George Hinde-Hayes was born. The month after his birth, he was christened in the village church of St John the Baptist, initially bearing only his father's surname but later incorporating his mother's maiden name of Hinde.

His father, Charles Hayes, described variously as an agricultural labourer, grazier and market gardener, had moved into the Hinde family home after marrying Elizabeth in 1881. Unusually, the couple had married fairly late with Charles being around 38 years old and Elizabeth being about 26.

The house was located on the Rugby Road, on the outskirts of the village. It had just four rooms and by the time of the 1891 Census, it was home to nine people. This not only included George and his parents but also his older brother, Charles, and younger sisters, Charlotte and Alice.

By the time of the 1901 Census, the family had moved to 51, Pinfold Street in the Bilton area of Rugby. Nevertheless, it seems that they were still living 'cheek by jowl', with ten of them living in this cramped four-room mid-terrace house. Although George's older brother, Charles, had by then moved out, the family had grown by a further two children. These were Frederick, ten, and Frank, who was four. George, by this time, was around 17 years old and working as a labourer at the nearby Rugby cement works.

The Military Cross (MC). (*Author's photo*)

By 1911, living conditions had improved greatly for the family as they had moved into 80, York Street in Rugby. Though still a mid-terrace house, it had two more rooms than their old house and the number of occupants had reduced dramatically, Now, it was just George, his parents and brothers, Frederick and Frank. On a personal level, it seems George's prospects had improved too as, rather than labouring at the local cement works, he was now a railway carter in the shunting yards at British Thompson Houston. As well as a site in Coventry, the company had a very large heavy engineering works in Rugby and was a major employer in the town.

On 27 April 1914, the month after their father died, George and his kid brother, Frank, decided to enlist with their local Territorial unit, the 7th Bn Royal Warwicks. At the time, George was 29 and Frank was just two days away from his seventeenth birthday, the minimum age at which a young man could enlist. George was allocated the service number 2215 and Frank received the number 2216. Just two months later, on 28 June, Archduke Franz Ferdinand and his wife were assassinated in Sarajevo, making war in Europe inevitable.

When war finally broke out on 28 July, the brothers quickly found themselves separated as George left with the battalion that August, for combat training at

Witham, Essex. Given that Frank was not eligible for overseas service due to his age, he subsequently became part of the 2/7 Royal Warwicks. This was a second line battalion that would initially remain in England to fulfil the home defence role. The purpose for which the territorials had originally been formed.

Having achieved the rank of Corporal, George sailed to France with his battalion on 22 March 1915. However, it would not be until 22 May 1916 that Frank, by then 19 years old, would eventually land in France to join the fighting.

It was on 19 July, just less than two months after Frank had arrived, that his battalion was involved in an assault on German positions, just a few kilometres south of Armentieres. The battalion was entrenched at Fauquissart and it was B and C Coys that went forward at 0600 hours that day to press the attack. By 0810 hours, the attack was over and what was left of the men began their withdrawal. By then, 13 officers and 305 NCO's and men had been killed. Frank, a soldier with B Coy, was one of those who never came back.

George must have been devastated by the news of Frank's death. But, as with many other soldiers who found themselves in such a terrible position, he had to fight on. Eventually, his service led him to the shattered fields just east of Ypres, where his own fate awaited. Of the many men of the battalion who advanced with such gallantry on the morning of 4 October 1917, George would be singled out for special recognition. It would be his exceptional bravery and skill that would later see him awarded a Military Cross (MC) for his actions as the battalion fought to defeat the enemy machine guns that awaited them. His citation reads thus:

> *For conspicuous gallantry and devotion to duty. The advance was held up by a strong enemy machine-gun position, and all the officers became casualties. He took command and crawled to a flank under direct fire from the post, to a position from which he killed several of the enemy. He then led his men in an attack on the post, which he captured, with ten prisoners and a machine gun. He showed splendid courage and initiative.*

Though George, through his actions, helped the battalion to achieve its objectives that day, it was also a day that ended with him being seriously wounded and evacuated to hospital. Six days later, at 14 General Hospital at Wimereux, close to Boulogne, George succumbed to his wounds and was buried at Wimereux Communal Cemetery.

The inscription on his headstone was requested by his mother, Elizabeth. She also received his savings of £16.3/9d, a war gratuity of £21.10/- and a weekly pension of 7/-. Though George was buried at Wimereux, Frank's body was never recovered from the battlefield and he is commemorated at the Loos Memorial to the missing. Both are honoured locally on the British Thompson Houston Memorial, which now stands at its new location in front of the old factory buildings on Technology Drive, Rugby.

William Hindle – Lance Corporal 202501

Died on 8 October 1917, aged 21.
Commemorated at Tyne Cot Memorial.
Panel 24.

Born in the second quarter of 1897, William was christened in the parish of Chorley on 13 June 1897. Although William Hindle's father, Joseph, was a railway worker, the rest of his family worked predominantly in the cotton mills of Lancashire. At the time, the industry was the premier employer in the area and the family was engaged in various roles, including William's mother, Alice Ann (nee Hart), who worked as a cotton weaver before becoming a full-time housewife.

A glance at the 1891 Census gives a very good idea of the sort of close-knit community that William was born into. It shows that different branches of both the Hart and Hindle family were living in Hope Street, Chorley, in cramped terraced houses typical of the working-class areas of Victorian towns and cities up and down the country. The 'stand out' occupation in the street at the time is that of Police Constable James Woods at number four. Of the other working-age occupants of the street, the vast majority were employed in the cotton mills in one capacity or another. Albeit Joseph, as previously mentioned, was by then a railway worker, later becoming a gateman for the Lancashire and Yorkshire Railway Company.

By the time of the 1901 Census, the family had moved from 8, Hope Street and had gone just a stone's throw around the corner to 3, Parker Street, moving next door to another branch of the Hindle family. By now, Joseph and Alice's family was complete and they had a total of seven children, all living together in another small, terraced house. William was the second youngest of the family, with Robert, 16, Peter, 12, Thomas, 11, and Hannah, five, being his older siblings. By that time William was three years old and the youngest of the family, Doris, was just two.

By the 1911 Census, the family had moved about half a mile away, to another terraced house, this time at 62, Harpers Lane. Much of the family was working, apart from Alice and Doris who, at 12 years old, was still at school, albeit on a part-time basis. Joseph was still working on the railway but the remaining children were all working in the cotton mills, including William who, at 13, was a spinning room creeler, keeping the looms fed with loose fibres to be turned into yarn.

Though William's service record does not exist, we do know that when he first enlisted, he joined his local territorial unit, the 1/4 Bn Loyal North Lancashire Regiment (Loyal North Lancs) as Private 3656 Hindle. A calculation based on the war gratuity received by his family indicates that he enlisted around September 1915, making him around 18 years old at that time.

William was reported as missing in action on 8 October 1917. However, there is no way of knowing whether he lost his life while serving on a working party that day, or whether that was the first opportunity to recognise him as missing since the attack commenced on the ground around Terrier Farm.

After William's death, his mother, Alice, received a war gratuity of £12.10/-, as well as his savings of £3.18/5d. She was also awarded a dependant's pension of 6/- a week, later rising to 10/6d. However, William's father, Joseph, died in July of 1918 and it seems that a few years later, Alice felt the need to make a new life for herself. In 1921 she emigrated to America, taking up residence in Rhode Island.

As well as his commemoration on the memorial wall of Tyne Cot Cemetery, William is commemorated on the Chorley Civic War memorial, located in the town's Astley Park. The memorial records the names of 572 Chorley men who lost their lives in the Great War.

William Thomas Houghton – Private 202847

Died of wounds on 4 October 1917, aged 32.
Buried at Mendinghem Military Cemetery.
Grave reference: VII. B. 29

Born in New Bilton, Warwickshire in the second quarter of 1885, William Houghton is another soldier from the Rugby area. His father, Joseph, was a shoemaker and originally from Northamptonshire. William was the youngest of six children who he raised with his wife, Annie.

Baptised in Rugby on 7 January 1887, William next appears in civic records in the 1891 Census. By then, he was six years old and the family were living at 23, Russell Street, Rugby. Though, from the details held in the record, it is clear that he was born much later than his siblings. Annie would have been around 40 years old when she gave birth to William, which was quite old for that time. The next youngest sibling was his brother, Frederick, who, at 13 years old and working as an errand boy, was seven years his little brother's senior. Next youngest was 14-year-old Emily, who was working as a domestic servant. Next followed Mary, who at 17 was working as a dress-stay maker, and finally older brother Harry, 19, was working as a railway clerk.

The 1901 Census has no record of William. Nevertheless, it is clear he had moved out of his parent's house by then as Annie and Joseph were at a new address in Rugby – 84, Rowland Street, and were looking after their seven-year-old granddaughter, Lilly.

In 1909, William married Laura Martha Brown in Rugby and a couple of years later, the 1911 Census records the couple living in Kilsby, a village around five miles southeast of Rugby. William was, by then, the live-in grocery manager at the Kilsby branch of the Co-Operative Society. The following year, on 12 March 1912, their family was complete with the birth of their daughter, Phyllis.

William's service record has not survived, so we do not have a precise date for his enlistment. It is known that he enlisted at Rugby and that this would not have been before early October 1916. However, with no surviving documents to shed light on his service, all we can say is that he was seriously injured during the first day of the Broodseinde offensive and died from those wounds later the same day. It is perhaps worthy of mention that, due to the incredible efficiency of the battlefield medical services, William was successfully evacuated to a CCS located in the village of Proven, around 15 miles from where he was first injured.

Originally, the village hosted the 46th (1/1 Wessex) CCS from July 1916. However, a further four CCSs were established in the village at the start of the

The War Memorial Gates, Rugby. (*Author's photo*)

third Ypres campaign. Consequently, Mendinghem Military Cemetery was established just beyond the village to receive the burials of those men who the respective stations were unable to save.

Perhaps it gave some comfort to Laura that her husband at least had a final resting place, unlike so many of his comrades. As for compensation for her loss, she received William's savings of 27/10d, a war gratuity of £3.00 and a weekly widow's pension of 20/5d, initially. Though, she was not officially informed of his death until 1 November.

As well as his gravestone, William's name is commemorated on the memorial gates at Whitehall Recreation Ground, Rugby. However, Laura herself ensured the creation of two more personal and heartfelt tributes to her husband, which she and William's family posted in the Rugby advertiser on 10 November. They read:

HOUGHTON.—In loving memory of my dear husband, Pte. W. T. HOUGHTON, 1/7th R.W. Regiment, who was killed in action on October 4, 1917, "somewhere in France" aged 32 years.

> "Sleep on, loved one, in your far-off grave:
> A grave I may never see;
> But as long as life and memory lasts
> We shall always remember thee."
> —From his sorrowing Wife and Child.

HOUGHTON.—In loving memory of Pte. W. T. HOUGHTON, 1/7th R.W. Regiment, who was killed in action on October 4, 1917.

> "Not dead to those who loved him,
> Not lost, but gone before;
> He lives with us in memory,
> And will for evermore."
> —From his sorrowing Mother, Brothers and Sisters.

His loving wife, Laura, passed away in Rugby in June 1922, aged just 36 years old. It is not known if she ever got the opportunity to visit William's grave.

Arthur Robert Howes – Private 29255 B Coy

Killed in action on 8 October 1917, aged 19 years.
Commemorated at Tyne Cot Memorial.
Panel 26.

Just a few miles east of Norwich in Norfolk lies the parish of Moulton. Located in the district of Blofield and in an area dependant on agriculture, it was here in 1898 that Arthur Howes was born. The son of Robert Howes, a traction engine driver, and Clara (nee Hinds), a farmer's daughter, Arthur was christened in the nearby village of Acle on 18 July 1898.

In 1901 Robert and Clara were living with Clara's father, Samuel Hinds, a 55-year-old farmer and a widower, who was also likely the employer of his son-in-law, Robert. As well as two-year-old Arthur, resident too was his older

Strumpshaw
war memorial.
(*Photo credit –
Adrian S Pye, War
Memorials Online*)

brother, Samuel, who was then five, and his one-year-old sister, Esther. Home itself was a four-roomed house in Blofield Road, in the village of Lingfield.

By 1911, the family had moved to a four-roomed home of their own – Mill House in Moulton. Robert was still driving agricultural traction engines and his oldest son, Samuel, was by then 15 and also working on farms as a labourer. Though at 12 years old, Arthur was not yet old enough to work and was still at school. The family had expanded by this time too, with two further daughters: Laura, seven, and Helen, two. However, the oldest Howes girl, Esther, is not on the 1911 Census record for the family home. Instead, she appears on the list of residential scholars at the Royal Deaf and Dumb Asylum for Children in Victoria Road, Margate.

Arthur's army record no longer exists, so all that can be established about the start of his service is that he enlisted at Norwich, sometime after early October 1916. Initially he served as Private 24761 Howes of the 3rd Bn The Norfolks. This was a reserve unit that remained in the UK throughout the war and was used as a training battalion. It would likely have been from here that Arthur was eventually sent to join his new unit, the 1/7 Royal Warwicks, at the front. Though, prior to this, he had already been issued with his new service number of 29255 and did not join a TF unit until after their renumbering in early 1917. Arthur subsequently fell in action on 8 October 1917 while serving in B Coy.

After his death, his father, Robert, received a war gratuity of £3.00 and his son's savings of £3.18/9d. Arthur nominated his mother, Clara, as the recipient of a dependant's pension of 4/12d a week. As his body was never recovered from the battlefield, his name is commemorated on the memorial wall at Tyne Cot cemetery. He is also remembered locally on the war memorial on the grounds of St Peter's Church, Norwich Road, Strumpshaw. The memorial bears the names of fourteen other men from the area who fell in the Great War.

Philip Harry Hunt – Private 27767

Died of wounds on 8 October 1917, aged 36.
Commemorated at Tyne Cot Memorial.
Panel 26.

A lifelong native of the town of Pershore in Worcestershire, Philip Hunt was born in July 1880. He was the youngest of eight children born to George Hunt, a painter, and Hannah (nee Lock), a laundress. Philip was just eight months old at the time he appears in the 1881 Census, which also records his four siblings then living under the same roof. They ranged in ages from Ernest, the next youngest, at four, to Rosa, six, and Sarah Ann, aged nine. The oldest child was Thomas, who at 16 was apprenticed to a cabinet maker.

Home for the family was Stanhope House, Bridge Street in Pershore. This was a very grand three-storey Georgian townhouse, built around 1780. However, by the time the Hunt family were resident, the building had seen better days and was divided into a house of multiple occupancy, with a number of other families also resident in the building. The house itself though eventually saw an upturn in its fortunes and still stands today as a Grade II listed building.

Although Thomas was the oldest of the children in the household, he was not the first of George and Hannah's children. Instead, records show that he had an older sister, Caroline, born around 1861. There

Pershore Abbey war memorial. (*Photographer unknown, War Memorials Online*)

was also Lilly, born around 1869, and William, born in 1871. Of the three children, William died at just one year old, Lilly later went to live with her aunt and uncle, and Caroline subsequently entered domestic service.

Caroline died at the relatively young age of around 45, in 1906. Her mother, Hannah, then died in January of 1908, with George dying one year after his wife, in the following January. The couple were 75 and 76 respectively, which were relatively good ages for working-class people at that time.

By the time of his parents' passing, Phillip, along with his brother, Ernest, had taken up their father's old trade of painting and the 1911 Census shows a change of address for the first time for Philip. No longer living at Stanhope House, he was now resident with his sister, Lilly, and her carpenter husband, William Collett, at their four-room home, Manor Cottage in Pershore. Although he was 30 by this time, Philip was still a bachelor.

As with so many soldiers from the Great War, Philip's service record no longer exists and any detailed information on his service is not therefore available. All that can be established is that he initially joined his local territorial unit, enlisting at Pershore in the 1/8 Worcestershire Regiment (The Worcesters) as Private 4881 Hunt. From there he was then transferred, first to the 11th and then the 14th Bn The Royal Warwicks, where he acquired the service number 27767. From there he has at some stage transferred to his final unit, the 1/7 Royal Warwicks.

Philip could have been serving on the Western Front as early as 1915, given that all three of his previous battalions were in France by that November at the latest. However, the only thing we can say for sure is that his service ended on 8 October 1917, when he died of his wounds. Given the fact that he is recorded as dying from wounds, it seems reasonable to assume that he did receive some form of treatment on or close to the battlefield and his body was then lost after either being left on the battlefield, or receiving a field burial, the location of which was either not recorded, or destroyed by shelling.

Ultimately, no records could be found to tell us who may have received his effects, or any dependant's pension. Philip's story can therefore only be concluded by adding that, as well as his name being added to the Tyne Cot memorial wall, he is also remembered locally on the war memorial inside Pershore Abbey. His name joins that of a further 100 men from the area who were lost in the Great War.

Harold George Hurdley – Private 268853

Killed in action on 4 October 1917, aged 23 years.
Commemorated at Tyne Cot Memorial.
Panel 26.

The only available records that outline the early life of Harold George Hurdley are the 1901 and 1911 Census returns and the index of births for 1894. These confirm that he was born in Broseley, Shropshire in the second quarter of that year. Curiously though, in both census records, he is referred to as 'George Harold', an anomaly that currently remains unexplained. He was the eldest of two children and the only son of George Hurdley and Clara (nee Churchman). His sister, Freda, was Harold's junior by a year.

Although Harold moved to Coventry before enlistment, the available records confirm that his parents remained resident at the same address where Harold grew up. This was 27, Church Street, Broseley, a modest terraced cottage, which still stands today. Harold's father worked in the town as a manufacturer's clerk at the firm of Maw & Co, which produced encaustic tiles. These were patterned ceramic tiles, predominantly for use on floors, which the firm manufactured until the closure of the factory in 1970.

Broseley war memorial.
(*Photo credit – Richard
Law, TracesofWar.Com*)

Harold's service record has survived; we therefore know that, prior to military service, he was living at 56, Stoney Stanton Road, Coventry and was working as a clerk. His medical examination notes record him as being 6' tall and of a 'fair' standard of physical development. He had a chest measurement of 34½", with a 3" expansion and weighed in at 144lbs.

Although he was attested in Coventry on 7 December 1915, he was placed on the reserve list until 24 April 1917, when he was finally enlisted and mobilised with the 1/7 Royal Warwicks. Having completed his basic training, Harold was transferred to the fighting strength of the BEF and on 3 August 1917, he embarked for France, sailing from Southampton.

Harold's introduction to life on the Western Front would certainly have been a baptism of fire. By 8 August, the battalion had been moved from a training camp up to positions by the Yser Canal, just outside Ypres. He would have had hardly any time to adjust to this deadly new environment before experiencing his first gas attack on 11 August, when the battalion was shelled with large quantities of mustard gas. From that point, he would spend the rest of the month engaged in operations with his battalion in the St Julien Sector. Here his new life would have been a constant cycle of front-line fighting, punctuated by withdrawal to rest areas and manning work parties.

This continued until the start of September, when the battalion withdrew to the village of Sint-Jan-ter-Biezen, just west of Poperinghe. Here, they began a month's intensive training in preparation for the Broodseinde offensive. It was the day after the battalion was relieved from that battlefield that George was fatally wounded and died.

After his death, his father, George, received his son's savings of £3.8/5d and a war gratuity of £3.00. His mother, Clara, would receive a dependant's pension but the information as to the amount she was awarded has not survived.

As one of the missing, George is commemorated on the Tyne Cot memorial wall. He is also remembered on Broseley's war memorial, located in High Street, along with 52 other men from the town who fell in the Great War.

John Robert Johnson – Private 29254

Killed in action on 8 October 1917, aged 33 years.
Commemorated at Tyne Cot Memorial.
Panel 26.

The oldest child of Robert and Rebecca (nee Russell), John 'Jack' Johnson was born in the April of 1884 in Ramsey St Mary, Huntingdonshire. This small parish lies north of the town of Huntingdon in the modern county of Cambridgeshire and is set in prime agricultural countryside. At the time of Jack's birth, farming was the chief method of employment in the area, with Jack's father, Robert, working as an agricultural labourer.

From the time of his birth, the family lived at Herne Road in Ramsey St Mary and Jack was followed by a further five siblings: James, William, Annie, Harold and Whitwell. All were born between 1886 and 1901.

By the time of the 1901 Census, 16-year-old Jack, along with his brothers, James and William, had found work and moved out of the family home. However, the young farm horse keeper and his brothers had not gone far and had instead moved into their grandparents' house, also in Herne Road.

In 1905, Jack's father, Robert, died before he could see his eldest son marry Mary Elizabeth Corney in 1907. However, the newly married couple's first year together would be tainted by sadness as they saw the birth and death of their daughter, Ada. The couple stayed close by to Jack's family, living in their own house in Herne Road until tragedy struck again when Mary died in 1913 at around 27 years old.

Having lost Mary, it would be a further two years before Jack found happiness once more when he married Martha Jane Corney, Mary's 23-year-old sister, at Huntingdon

Private John 'Jack' Robert Johnson during his service with the Norfolk Regiment. (*Public domain*)

in June of 1915. That following month, Martha and Jack would welcome their only child into the world, a daughter named Ivy who subsequently lived to the age of 97, passing away in Peterborough in 2012.

Although it is not clear when exactly Jack enlisted, it is known that he joined up at Huntingdon, joining the 7th (Service) Bn, The Norfolks as Private 27493 Johnson. The unit was part of Kitchener's New Army and was formed in Norwich in August 1915. This battalion was in France by the end of May 1915, but Jack is unlikely to have enlisted with them before October 1916.

Jack's service record has not survived and it is not therefore known when he transferred over to the 1/7 Royal

Jack Johnson's second wife, Martha Jane, nee Corney. (*Public domain*)

Warwicks. The only certain thing known of his service, therefore, is that he was killed in action on 8 October 1917. As his widow, Martha received a war gratuity of £3.00. She also received Jack's savings of £2.8/- and a weekly pension of 20/5d. Martha also lost her brother, Edward, the following March. He was serving with the 20th Hussars when he was killed in action near Jussy, France. Martha passed away in Peterborough in 1977 having remarried to Cecil Wood in 1921.

John, 'Jack' Johnson is remembered on the memorial wall at Tyne Cot cemetery. He is also remembered on the commemorative plaque erected in St Mary's Church, at Ramsey St Mary and on the stone memorial cross erected in Ramsey town. The latter contains the names of a further 144 men from the area who also fell in the Great War.

Arthur Manders – Private 201057

Killed in action on 4 October 1917, aged 19 years.
Commemorated at Tyne Cot Memorial.
Panel 26.

Establishing the details of Arthur Manders' early years proved problematic and his story eventually needed to be traced from when his father, Walter, married Clara Beatrice Wheeler. She was a native of Bridgewater, Somerset and they wed in Bristol on 25 January 1890.

When records for the couple next appear, in the 1891 Census, Walter was earning his living as a labourer. Home was House 4, Court 4, 37, Saltley Road, Aston in Birmingham. Now long demolished and replaced by industrial units, the only structure the Manders family would probably recognise today would be the iron Victorian railway bridge that now spans the modern dual carriageway. The building was typical of the cramped accommodation available throughout the vast working-class areas of Birmingham and sharing the house with them was their lodger, Louise Dowler. She had two young daughters: Alice, four, and Annie, two.

Arthur's birth is subsequently recorded as being in Aston during the second quarter of 1898. He then appears in the census records for 1901. However, home was not Aston but 37, Broad Street, Bromsgrove, where he lived with his grandfather, John Manders, his grandmother, Mary, and the couple's eight children. Though, neither of Arthur's parents are listed as living there too.

Instead, the 1901 Census suggests that Walter and Clara appeared to be living separately. Walter is on record as staying with his uncle, Henry, in Coalville, Leicestershire and working as a general labourer. However, Clara does not appear in the census records for the year, so it remains unclear whether she was living close to Arthur, or to her husband.

It is only by the time the 1911 Census comes around that Arthur is finally linked on record to both of his parents when the family are recorded as living in three rooms at 11, Drury Lane, Birmingham. By then, Walter was working as a stoker for a spade maker. The record also shows that Arthur, by then 13, actually has two older sisters: Emily, who was 17 and working as a silver plater, and 16-year-old Laura, an umbrella maker. He also had a ten-year-old brother, Sidney, and both boys are recorded as being at school.

There are no records available to tell us if Arthur ever took up any sort of trade prior to his enlistment in the army. However, because the record of his war gratuity payment still exists, it is possible to calculate that he likely enlisted in the early half of 1915. The available army records also show that this was in Birmingham and that he initially served with the 8th Bn Royal Warwicks. It is therefore likely that his enlistment took place at their HQ at Aston Barracks. If the calculations for enlistment are correct, this would have made Arthur around 17 years old when he took the King's Shilling.

Miscellaneous MOD documents aside, Arthur's actual service record no longer exists and therefore there is no way of knowing whether he was found out to be underage when he first joined his unit on active service or indeed which unit that was with. Arthur's service number is part of the batch allocated to the 7th Bn Royal Warwicks, so it confirms that he was with them by the time they were renumbered in early 1917. However, there is no way of telling when Arthur was actually transferred from the 8th to the 7th Battalion. The only certainty as to his actual service is that he would eventually be lost in combat on the first day of the Battle of Broodseinde.

As Arthur's sole legatee, his mother, Clara, received her son's savings of 12/8d and a war gratuity payment of £12.10/-. She was also awarded a pension of 6/6d a week.

Arthur has no known grave and so his name is remembered on the memorial wall at Tyne Cot Cemetery. Though a war memorial cross exists in Aston, Arthur's name has not been included and it is not known whether he is commemorated locally elsewhere.

Alfred Maynard – Private 266093

Died on 8 October 1917, aged 21 years.
Commemorated at Tyne Cot Memorial.
Panel 26.

Alfred Maynard was the sixth son of Robert Maynard; a gas works stoker, and his wife, Martha (nee Drinkwater).

Born in Stratford-upon-Avon in 1896, his upbringing was typically working class. At the time of the 1901 Census, the family lived at 27, Mansell Street and along with Alfred and his parents were five other brothers. At 13, Henry was the oldest and working as an errand boy. Then there was William, aged nine, and Edward, seven. At five years old, Alfred was senior to his youngest brother, Hubert, who was just one year old.

In 1904, older brother Henry passed away, but by the time of the 1911 Census, another brother, not mentioned in the 1901 Census, was then resident in the family home. This was Robert, a 21-year-old gardener. William was now working as a labourer for the local corporation, Edward as an ironmonger and Alfred, at 16, was working as a printer's errand boy. Hubert was still at school by this time but the family had also grown, with the addition of Alice, nine, Archibald, eight days' and three-year-old Gertrude.

Although the family had stayed in Mansell Street, they were now living at number 18. This tiny terraced cottage still exists today and is located in the town centre, not far from William Shakespeare's birthplace. It comprised just four rooms and was clearly a very cramped space for a family of ten.

Alfred's enlistment as Private 5269 Maynard into 10th (Service) Bn Royal Warwicks took place at Birmingham Town Hall on 3 September 1914. At

Stratford-upon-Avon war memorial. (*Author's photo*)

the time, he claimed to be 19 years and nine months old. Clearly, Alfred had added a year to his age to ensure acceptance as he signed up to a three-year short service attestation.

A glimpse of the then young labourer can be gleaned from his medical exam notes where the officer completing noted that Alfred was of fair complexion with auburn hair and grey eyes. He is recorded as standing at 5'.5½" tall and weighing a healthy 126lbs. His faith is recorded as Church of England.

However, all did not go well with Alfred's new career and he was subsequently discharged on 24 September under Para 392 (iii) (c) of King's Regulations as 'not likely to become an efficient soldier'. The more specific reason given for this was defective eyesight. Therefore, after just twenty-one days' service, Alfred was discharged home from Tidworth Barracks.

Unfortunately, the only section of Alfred's service record to survive are just those few pages that document his initial attestation and discharge. There is therefore nothing else that reveals when he rejoined the Colours, or any detail of his later service, or how and when he came to serve with the 1/7 Royal Warwicks. The only thing for certain is that, as with many of his comrades, he had received a six-figure service number from a block allocated to the battalion. This means that Alfred was with the unit from at least the spring of 1917.

Alfred was not the only Maynard brother to join the army. Records show that William also enlisted around the first half of 1915 and served as Private 11421 Maynard with the 11th (Service) Bn The Royal Warwicks. He was later killed during the Battle of the Ancre on 16 November 1916, falling in action near the village of Beaumont Hamel in the Somme Sector. Though no specific marriage records could be found, William's effects and pension records do state that he left a widow, Rose. With no contemporary records to rely on, some further research via the 1939 England and Wales Register did reveal a widow by the name of Rose Maynard, living in Stratford and born in 1891. Rose is listed as a domestic char lady, as is her daughter, Rose Jnr, who was born on 18 April 1915, just around the time William went off to war. Though entirely plausible to suggest that this is the family William left behind, it is by no means a certainty and the link remains unproven.

It would be less than a year later that the Maynard family would experience yet more tragedy as Alfred too would fall in battle on 8 October 1917. As sole legatee, his mother, Martha, received a war gratuity of £13.10/- and his savings of £9.12/11d. She was also awarded a pension of 7/6d a week.

As neither of the Maynard brothers' remains were located for burial, they were commemorated along with the names of other missing soldiers, with

William's name added to the Thiepval Memorial on The Somme and Alfred's added to the memorial wall at Tyne Cot. Both men are also commemorated locally on the Great War Memorial Cross, which is located in the Garden of Remembrance in Old Town, Stratford-upon-Avon.

Vincent Miller – Private 306949

Died on 8 October 1917, aged 25 years.
Commemorated at Tyne Cot Memorial.
Panel 27A.

It is fortunate that Vincent Miller's service record was not among those destroyed during World War Two, as absolutely no records have been located to tell us about his life prior to the 1911 Census. Furthermore, the opportunity to learn about his remarkable service history would have been lost to us.

From his army record and the 1911 Census, it is possible to ascertain that he was born in the Manchester area, specifically Longsight, around 1892. The census adds to this by recording that Vincent was the head of the household at 4, Brougham Street, West Gorton. Resident with him were his 15-year-old sister, Mary, and four of his relatives from the Brennan family: nephew Michael, 7, and nieces Kate, 19, Edie, ten, and Sarah, eight. At the time, Vincent was working as a carter and Mary was a housemaid in an infirmary. However, there are no details of where his mother, Catherine McGinn, lived prior to this time. His army record only confirms that Vincent's father was deceased at the time he enlisted. His name is therefore unknown.

Vincent joined the 8th Territorial Bn (Ardwicks), The Manchester Regiment (The Manchesters) on 11 February 1914 as Private 2019 Miller. At the time, the unit was based at their HQ in Ardwick Green, Manchester and Vincent was working as a machine hand for Brookes and Doxey in West Gorton. The firm manufactured machinery for the cotton spinning industry.

His attestation form has him as living at 23, Brougham Street, a few doors away from his old address, and describes him as 21 years old, 5′ 5½″ tall, with a 36½″ chest and 2½″ expansion. His physical development is recorded as fair and his faith as Roman Catholic.

When Britain declared war on Germany on 4 August 1914, Vincent's battalion was mobilised immediately and moved to camp at Hollingworth Lake, near Rochdale. Then, on 10 September 1914, the battalion boarded the SS *Corsican* at Southampton, bound for Alexandria in Egypt.

The unit would not stay long for their first tour in Egypt and subsequently crossed to Cyprus on 19 October to take part in the annexation of the island, before returning to Alexandria on 18 January 1915. After then moving to Cairo, the battalion engaged in training in the desert outside the city in preparation for the Gallipoli campaign.

The 8th Manchesters subsequently landed at Gallipoli on 6 May 1915. However, Vincent was not with his comrades during the landings as he had previously sustained a gunshot injury to his hand. This not only prevented him serving in the campaign but also saw him repatriated to England for treatment.

On 13 November 1915, Vincent was granted home leave and the record confirms that this was from 1 Southern General Hospital, Birmingham, for one week. His home address was given as 41, Margaret Street, West Gorton, which is recorded as his mother's address in later records.

Eventually, Vincent resumed full duties and was transferred to the 2/8 Royal Warwicks on 15 March 1916. He was then shipped out to France on 22 May 1916, landing at Le Havre.

Unfortunately, it would not be long before Vincent was wounded again. This time on 25 August 1916, when his unit was based at Bailleul. It appears that Vincent was part of B Coy, which staged a trench raid on that date. One of a number of men reported as wounded and missing, Vincent was shot in the face. Initially, he was evacuated to a nearby CCS with a bullet wound to his cheek, before being transferred to hospital in Boulogne. There he remained until rejoining his unit at Laventie on 14 September.

It seems that Vincent's fortunes improved little over the coming months. Initially, he fell foul of army regulations at the end of February 1917. Having been found to be deficient of tea and sugar from his iron rations, he was fined three days' pay. However, worse was to come when, on 9 April, he was again wounded, receiving a flesh wound from a bullet to his left thigh. Vincent may have felt that he had got off lightly with the flesh wound and remained in the field. But, just two days later, he was hit again. This much more serious injury was another gunshot wound to the head and would ultimately see him hospitalised, repatriated and then, in May, sent to Ballyvonare Camp in County Cork, Ireland. Here he would convalesce and receive rehabilitation treatment, before to returning to England.

While back in England, on 15 August 1917, Vincent was posted to the reserve for the 7th Bn The Royal Wawricks. From there, he was assigned to the 2/7 Royal Warwicks, returning to France on 8 September 1917. Here he joined his new unit, again based at Laventie. But, only nine days later, Vincent was transferred once more, this time joining the 1/7 Royal Warwicks as they completed training at Sint-Jan-ter-Biezen, Belgium. It would be just a few weeks later, on 8 October, that he was initially reported as missing in action outside Ypres, later being presumed killed.

As his sole legatee, Vincent's mother, Catherine McGinn, received her son's savings of £5.00 and a war gratuity of £14.10/-. She also received a dependant's pension of 12/6d a week.

As Vincent's remains were never recovered from the battlefield, he is commemorated at Tyne Cot memorial. It is not known if he is commemorated locally but his name does not appear on the Gorton and Abbey Hey District War Memorial, which lists the names of 117 men from the area who were recorded as killed or missing in the Great War.

Richard Francis Morritt – Private 266912

Killed in action on 8 October 1917, aged 26 years.
Commemorated at Tyne Cot Memorial.
Panel 27A.

Born in Liversedge, Yorkshire on 28 April 1891, Richard Morritt was just 1 month old when his name was recorded in the census for that year. His father, Francis Henry Morritt, was then a 27-year-old clerk and his mother, Jessie (nee Beckett), was 28 years old.

By the time of the 1901 Census, Richard had been joined by two brothers and a sister. These were Eric, the next oldest, aged seven, Gilbert, who was three, and baby Jessie, who was just three months old. Francis was still working as a clerk for a firm of fruit merchants and home by then was 2, Upper Exley, situated in a small rural community on the outskirts of Halifax.

It seems that Richard developed an early interest in military service and by 1908, while working as a labourer, he joined his local territorial unit. On 27 June of that year, 17-year-old Richard became Private 345 Morritt of the 4th Bn, West Riding Regiment (The West Ridings) and his attestation sheet records that he signed up for a term of four years. The year after he joined up, his father died. But Richard went on to finish his four-year term, completing annual camps at Redcar, Marske by Sea, the Isle of Man and Ripon. In the last year of his four-year term, he was promoted to lance corporal and also signed on for another year's service. The 1911 Census also confirms that Richard was by then living and working in the Poor Law Infirmary, Halifax, as a stores porter.

At some point after finishing his service with The West Ridings, Richard moved to the Midlands, which is where he next appears on record. This was on 27 April 1916, sometime after the outbreak of war, when he is again attested for service. This time it was at Dudley, in the Black Country. Initially, he was given the service number 5074 and enlisted into a reserve unit, the 3/7 Royal

Warwicks. At the time, he was working as a storekeeper and living in Burton Road, Dudley.

Richard's attestation and medical took place the day before his twenty-fifth birthday and he was recorded as being 5′ 9″ tall, having a 40½″ chest with a 4½″ expansion. He weighed in at 181lbs and was of good physical development.

On 10 September 1916, with his basic training completed, Richard was sent to France where he joined the 1/7 Royal Warwicks as part of C Coy. At the time, the battalion was in training and billeted at Authieule, a village just east of Gezaincourt. However, it would not be long before Richard sustained an injury that would trouble him for the remainder of his service. The date was 19 November 1916 and the battalion had provided a working party of 200 men engaged in the construction of a new HQ at Bazentin le Petit. It was here Richard sustained a sprain to his right ankle, so severe that he needed to report to the local field ambulance unit and was kept out of service until 15 December. Clearly, the sprain had caused a substantial weakness, as his right ankle would give way on two more occasions.

The next occurrence was on 15 February 1917, when the battalion was engaged in operations on the front line, close to Biaches and Iglau. The next was on 15 August, when the battalion was on operations outside of Ypres. At the time, they had just moved to Dambre Camp and were preparing to move up to the Yser Canal for an attack. Conditions at the time were recorded as wet and muddy and this latest injury kept Richard out of the field for a few more days.

The medical officer's report from the February injury still exists and it noted that Richard's condition was of a 'trivial' nature and unlikely to affect his 'future efficiency as a soldier'. For Richard, this meant that he would never receive the rehabilitative treatment that he probably needed. His subsequent return to duty would lead to his initially being reported missing on 8 October, later to be presumed killed in action.

Richard had never married and as his sole legatee, it was his mother, Jessie, who received his savings of 18/4d and a war gratuity payment of £7.1/8d. She also received a weekly dependant's pension, although the amount is not recorded. A civil probate record also exists for Richard's estate, dated 13 November 1918, in Wakefield. It records that Jessie received her son's remaining effects of £195.16/3d.

As his body was never recovered, Richard is commemorated on the memorial wall at Tyne Cot Cemetery. It is not known whether his name is recorded on any local memorials.

Thomas Naseby – Private 34004

Died on 8 October 1917, aged 34 years.
Commemorated at Tyne Cot Memorial.
Panel 27A.

Born in Bromley by Bow, Middlesex on 1 April 1883, Thomas Naseby was the sixth child of railway signalman Henry and his wife, Emily (nee Pratt). Although born and resident in Bow, an area of London, Thomas was actually christened on 9 September 1883, in the parish church of West Haddon. This was a village around eleven miles to the west of Northampton and where his father, Henry, had been born as part of the wider Naseby family, long established in the area.

Although too early to record Thomas, the 1881 Census shows Henry and Emily living with their young family in Bow. By which time Henry was 31 and Emily, 27. The Naseby's children by that time were Henry, seven, Ada, five, Harriet, four, Fred, three and George, one. A later school admissions record confirms that Thomas started school at Knapp Road School, Tower Hamlets, London on 6 December 1887. The document also records that the family's address by that time was 47, Sherwood Street and that his father had registered him at the school.

The 1891 Census has the family living at 116, Dace Road, Bow and with a further two children, Gerty and Walter, adding to the family. By this time Henry was working as a labourer and described as a widower. Emily, it transpires, had died in the early part of 1891, likely from consumption (tuberculosis). Henry had therefore employed a 62-year-old widow, Maria Dugard, as a live-in nurse for the children.

Inevitably, although he later remarried, Henry struggled to cope with caring for his children and eventually decided to place Thomas and Walter into the care of Dr Barnardo's children's home. Though Walter would not live long enough to leave the care of the home, Thomas eventually left in 1900 to take up work as a printer.

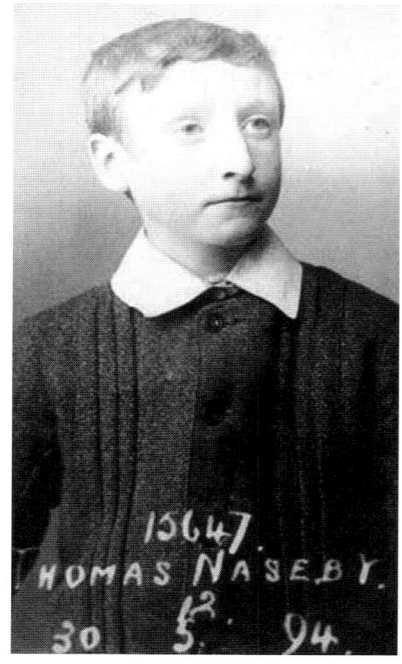

Thomas Naseby on admission to Dr Barnardo's. (*Public domain*)

The census for the following year records Thomas as living with his older sister, Ada, and her husband, Samuel Mills, at 24 Elizabeth Road, Upton Park in London. His occupation is recorded as being a printer's machine minder.

It seems that significant changes took place in Thomas's life in the years between the census of 1901 and 1911. Within this time, Thomas married Elizabeth (nee Elstob) on 25 December 1909 at St Stephen's, Church of England, in Upton Park. The couple also became the sole occupants of 24, Elizabeth Road, with sister Ada and her husband having moved elsewhere. The address itself, a comfortable-looking, five-roomed terraced house in a pleasant neighbourhood, still stands today.

Thomas Naseby and his bride, Elizabeth Elstob. (*Public domain*)

The couple soon became parents themselves and the first of two children, Evelyn, was born on 25 September 1911. Then their son, Stanley, was born on 24 September 1914, just a short time after the outbreak of war.

Thomas's service record no longer exists. There is therefore no certainty as to the details of where he served and when he first took part in the fighting on the Western Front. However, it is known that he enlisted into a territorial unit at East Ham, between September and October 1916. Originally Private 202006 Naseby of the 4th Bn The Buffs, he was subsequently transferred to the 1/7 Royal Warwicks, having previously been given the service number of 34004. Thomas was subsequently reported as missing in action, presumed dead on 8 October 1917.

Thomas's sole legatee was his widow, Elizabeth. She received his effects of £2.16/3d, a war gratuity payment of £3.10/- and a weekly dependant's pension of 25/5d. She later moved out of London, along with her parents and children, to live in Leigh on Sea, Essex.

As one of the missing, Thomas's name is commemorated on the memorial wall at Tyne Cot. He is also commemorated locally on the roll of honour kept in All Saints Church, in his family's home village of West Haddon.

Alfred Parrock – Private 266947

Died on 4 October 1917, aged 21 years.
Commemorated at Tyne Cot Memorial.
Panel 27.

Alfred Parrock was born in Worcestershire in 1896. The locations quoted are Cradley and Lye, though no birth records can be found to confirm either the location or exact date. He was registered as the only son of Joseph and Henrietta (nee Wallens) and the research into his story posed some intriguing questions that, circumstantially at least, now appear to have been answered.

Alfred first appears in the public record in the census of 1901. At the time, the family were living at 3, Brick Kiln, Quarry Bank, Staffordshire and Alfred was five years old. However, his parents were quite old to have a child of that age, even though Alfred is clearly listed as theirs. Joseph, a millwright by trade, was by then 54 and Henrietta was 55.

The 1911 Census again confirms the relationship and records Alfred as 15 and working in a warehouse for a cog manufacturer. By that time, the family had moved to 14, Vicarage Road, in Lye, Stourbridge and had taken in two lodgers: Lester Holt and John Nott. Usefully, the record sheet for 1911 does contain additional headings, which provide more information than in previous surveys. It therefore also records that the Parrocks had been married for forty-one years, yet had no children either born or surviving, strongly indicating that Alfred was not a blood relation and may have been adopted by the couple.

The next time Alfred appears on record is on 17 June 1913 when, at 17 years and seven months old, he enlisted at Stourbridge with his local territorial unit, the 1/7 Worcesters, as Private 2030 Parrock. Upon attestation Alfred again confirms working as a warehouseman, specifically for Henry Wooldridge, a cog manufacturer, of The Lawns, Hagley Road, Stourbridge. He gave his address as 3, Balls Lane, Wollescote and listed his mother, Henrietta, resident at the same address, as his next of kin. His medical record describes him as standing at 5′ 2½″ tall, of good vision and physical development and having a 32½″ chest with a 2″ expansion.

Alfred remained with D Coy of his battalion until 20 of June 1915, when he was posted to the 82nd Provisional Battalion, which was a reserve unit for the Gloucestershire Regiment (The Gloucesters) and engaged in home service only at that time. On 28 April 1916, he was discharged from that service 'subject to the provisions of the Military Service Act, 1916'. This meant that he could then be called up for military service overseas, which, as a member of the territorial force, he was not obliged to do if he had not signed the relevant waiver.

However, the very next day, he enlisted again at Worcester, in the 3/7 Royal Warwicks – this time as Private 5145 Parrock. The 20-year-old tool maker was passed A1 fit for service and described as being 5′ 6½″ tall with a 36″ chest and 3″ chest expansion. Again, he listed his mother, Henrietta, as his next of kin and resident at 3, Balls Lane, Wollescote.

While Alfred's service record confirms that he joined his battalion in the field on 29 August 1916, it is unclear which unit he joined as the relevant service sheet still only notes him as part of the reserve for the 7th Bn RWR. Although the nature of the training is not listed, he is next recorded as joining a course of instruction with IV Corps from 2 August 1917. He then joined the 1/7 Royal Warwicks on active service in the Ypres sector on 4 September and was killed in action on 4 October – the first day of the Battle of Broodseinde.

The probable facts around Alfred's early life only began to emerge once further research was carried out in relation to the payment of his effects and pension. Initially, it was noted that, despite Henrietta being previously recorded as Alfred's next of kin, the disbursement of his effects and war gratuity were made to a man variously referred to as A M Yardley, Alfred Major Yardley and Major Yardley. In the effects register, it is Yardley who is confusingly referred to as Alfred's father. As such he received Alfred's savings of £4.6/2d and a war gratuity payment of £6.00. Though, in order to receive those payments, Alfred would have had to personally nominate Yardley as his sole legatee.

The additional research that this prompted initially established that both Joseph and Henrietta had died in 1918, the year following Alfred's death. Joseph died on 10 January and Henrietta passed away on 6 April. In addition, authority to pay Alfred's effects to Yardley had only been granted on 18 March 1918. Payment of the gratuity to him was not authorised until 12 November 1919.

Interestingly, documents found later in Alfred's service record contain further next of kin entries, this time recording 'Major Parrock' as his father and next of kin. It also records a 21-year-old blood sister, Henrietta Yardley. Both of whom were then residing at 3, Balls Lane, Wollescote. A document listing next of kin, dated 7 February 1920, then listed Major Yardley as Alfred's father once more, along with Henrietta as his sister. This time, both are resident at 29, Bromley Street, Lye.

Matters finally gained further clarity when Major Yardley was discovered on the 1911 Census. Listed as a 37-year-old widower and working as a dray man, he was living with his parents and 13-year-old daughter, Henrietta, in Stourbridge. From there, it was possible to connect Major to Clara Yardley (nee Morris). She had married Major at Stourbridge in 1895 and later given birth to Henrietta in 1898, some two years after Alfred had been born. Clara had died in 1906, leaving Major as a widower. Those facts allowed for the most likely assumption that Alfred had been put up for adoption, prior to the birth of his sister, and had subsequently been taken in by the Parrocks, who lived in the same area as his birth family. Whatever the truth of it, Major did later apply for a dependant's pension, though it was subsequently refused as no prior dependency by Major upon Alfred could be established.

With no known grave, Alfred Parrock is commemorated alongside his fallen comrades on the memorial wall at Tyne Cot cemetery. It is not known whether he is commemorated on any local war memorials.

Horace A Pettit – Private 300072

Died of wounds on 10 October 1917, aged 19 years.
Buried at St. Sever Cemetery Extension, Rouen.
Grave reference: P. III. F. 11A.

Despite efforts to uncover some detail relating to Horace Pettit, there is very little that can be said about his life. The only civic records relating to him are the 1901 and 1911 Census's. Nothing could be found in relation to his birth or baptism and his mother's details are unknown.

From the 1901 Census, Horace is recorded as being born in West Dereham, a small village located deep in rural Norfolk. Given his age, this would have been around 1898. The record shows that he was then living with his father, John, a 32-year-old agricultural labourer, and his 14-year-old sister, Violet. All three are in turn living with John's parents. His grandfather, also John, is recorded as a 60-year-old wheelwright, and his grandmother, Mary, was 67.

By 1911, Horace had turned 13 and was working as a farm labourer, as was his father. Both grandparents, John and Mary, were still alive and head of the household John, at 76, was still working as a carpenter. However, by this time, Violet was not recorded on the census form and does not seem to be recorded in either death records, or that year's census.

Because Horace's service record no longer exists, the details of his military service also remain sketchy. Though, it is known that he enlisted at Downham Market in Norfolk and joined The Norfolks, serving as Private 201230 Pettit. What is also certain is that Horace would have enlisted before 4 August 1914 and had undertaken to serve overseas, prior to 30 September 1914. This is because these are the basic qualifying criteria for the award of the Territorial Force War Medal – a medal with which he had been issued. This is the rarest of the campaign medals from the Great War, with only 33,944 issued. However, given the fact that Horace was born in 1898, the awarding criteria for the medal also means that he could have only been around 16 when he enlisted and was therefore underage.

The fact that Horace was issued with a six-figure service number while with the Norfolk Regiment confirms that he was a member of the 11th Bn, when the territorial infantry was renumbered in the spring of 1917. He then transferred at some stage after this period and was issued with a further six-figure service number, 300072, which was part of the batch allocated to the 1/7 Royal Warwicks.

No records exist to confirm how and when Horace was wounded. It is also impossible to say which hospital he was admitted to after being evacuated from the front line. This is because, after he passed away on 10 October, he was buried at St Sever Cemetery Extension in Rouen. This cemetery served eight general hospitals, five stationary and a Red Cross hospital. Consequently, given that very few patient records exist from that time, it is not even possible to establish at which hospital Horace was a patient.

After Horace's death, it was his grandmother, Mary, who received his savings of £8.17/5d and a war gratuity of £14.10/-. As one final missing piece of the story of Horace's life, no records could be found to indicate whether a dependant's pension had been granted to any of his relatives.

Horace lies in St Sever Cemetery, Rouen, located under grave reference: P. III. F. 11A. His headstone carries no personal inscription from his family. He is also remembered in his home parish of West Dereham, where his name is inscribed on the base of a rough granite cross, along with fifteen other men of the parish who fell in the Great War. The cross is located in the churchyard of St Andrew's Church, West Dereham.

Thomas Phillips – Private 268206

Died on 4 October 1917, aged 28 years.
Commemorated at Tyne Cot Memorial.
Panel 27A.

Born in Aston, Birmingham in the first quarter of 1890, Thomas Phillips was baptised at All Saints parish on 9 March of the same year. He was the first-born son of Thomas, a jeweller's engraver, and his wife, Mary Jane.

The 1891 Census lists the family as living at 154, Burbury Street, Aston, which was a small, two-up two-down, terraced house. The house would have been comfortable enough at the time to have housed the couple, who by then only had Thomas and their second son, Arthur, who is recorded as being less than six months old. Sadly, it appears Arthur died the following year as two deaths in that name are recorded for July and September of 1892, including one in Aston.

By the 1901 Census, the family had moved to 144, Lennox Road, which was also in Aston and home to many others employed in the nearby jewellery quarter and brass goods manufacturing workshops. By then, the family had grown with the addition of 7-year-old Ernest, and daughters, Ida, five, and Ivy, three.

The 1911 Census records a further change of house, this time to 82, Brunswick Road in the Handsworth area of the city. Located close to the jewellery quarter, this terraced house, slightly bigger than the previous homes, still stands today. While Thomas Snr was still carrying on his profession as an engraver, young Thomas, at 21 years old, was by then earning his keep as an insurance agent for the Prudential Assurance Company. Ernest, at 17, was working too, as a scale maker, and Ida, at 15, was also contributing to the family income by working as a milliner.

Thomas's service record still exists and initially it can be seen that he had already been in service with the TF. Though the record is somewhat illegible in relation to this, it can be made out that he was previously a member of HQ Coy of the Army Service Corps (ASC), possibly based at Stafford, and that he was discharged from that unit in 1905. Thomas then enlisted into another territorial unit when he went to the Suffolk Street Recruiting Office in Birmingham and enlisted with the Warwickshire Yeomanry as Private 3504 Phillips. His attestation date is recorded as being on 25 November 1915 and service commenced immediately as he was embodied on the same date.

His medical notes record the 25-year-old as being 5′ 8″ tall, weighing 154lb and with a 38″ chest with a 2″ expansion. His physical development was described as good.

Thomas would remain in the UK with the Yeomanry for around thirteen months. At which point, on 23 December 1916, he was transferred to the 5th Bn Royal Warwicks and issued with the new service number, 8408. The very next day, Christmas Eve, he was on a ship from Southampton, bound for Le Havre, before disembarking on Christmas Day to join his unit in the field. However, Thomas's record does not say whether he was in the 1/5 or 2/5 Royal Warwicks, both of which were on active service in France with different infantry divisions by the time of his arrival at the front. There is therefore no way of knowing where precisely he served on the Western Front before his transfer to the 1/7 Royal Warwicks.

Thomas's transfer came swiftly, on 12 January 1917, and he was again renumbered, this time as Private 20463. At the time he transferred, his new battalion was engaged in an extended period of training and billeted around Allery and Mericourt, France. In early February they moved to the front lines at Eclusier, close to the Somme River and canal where severely low temperatures had not only caused the canal to freeze, but also sections of the river.

The battalion remained on operations in the Somme sector, during which time the men were renumbered and Thomas was issued with his final service number, 268206. They then moved into Belgium and into the Ypres sector on 23 July where they trained for and then engaged in the third Battle of Ypres.

Thomas Phillips was killed in action on 4 October 1917, the first day of the Battle of Broodseinde, at 28 years of age. He bequeathed his savings of £4.3/5d to his father, who also received a war gratuity of £8.10/-. His mother, Mary Jane, received a dependant's pension, albeit the surviving record cards do not record the amount.

In the year following Thomas's death, his brother, Ernest, enlisted with the RAF at Birmingham on 30 May, becoming Airman 189946 Phillips. Ernest survived the war and passed away in Birmingham in January 1959.

Thomas's remains were never recovered from the battlefield and he is therefore commemorated on the memorial wall at Tyne Cot Cemetery. It is not known if he is commemorated on any local memorials, though a number are still known to exist in the Aston area of Birmingham. However, he is commemorated on a stunning bronze and stone memorial, dedicated to those employees of the Prudential Assurance Company who fell in the Great War. The memorial still stands at its original location, outside the company's former head office in Waterhouse Square, High Holborn, London.

Cecil Peter Stanley Postle – Private 300074

Killed in action on 4 October 1917, aged 22 years.
Commemorated at Tyne Cot Memorial.
Panel 27A.

Born in Burlingham, Norfolk on 9 October 1894, Cecil Postle was the oldest son of a wheelwright, Edgar Peter Postle, and his wife, Sarah Ann (nee Cooper). He was preceded by two sisters, Stella and Alice, and was the older brother of Edwin and Albert.

Baptised in the parish of Caistor with Markshall on 1 August 1897, Cecil and his family are recorded in the 1901 Census, with Stella and Alice being ten and eight years old, respectively, and Edwin and Albert listed as four and two years old. Home was the village of Shotesham, just a few miles south of Norwich. The area itself was deep in rural Norfolk and, other than the local publican, all the family's neighbours were engaged in agricultural roles of one form or another.

By the time of the 1911 Census, the family had moved to the village of Newton Flotman, a larger community but still rural and this time located to the east of Norwich. By then, Stella and Alice were no longer living in the family home and Edwin and Albert were then aged 14 and 12 respectively. Both Cecil, by then 16, and Edwin are shown as working, though their occupation has not been recorded. However, it would probably be safe to assume that they were both engaged in agriculture in some way.

Cecil's service record has not survived, so any great detail as to his army career is not available. What is known is that he enlisted at Norwich, probably sometime in April 1916, joining The Norfolks as Private 6197 Postle. However, his actual battalion is currently unknown. Equally, there is no information to say when he first landed in France, or when he was posted to the 1/7 Royal Warwicks. The only certainty there is that he was clearly with the battalion when new service numbers were issued, given that his number is part of the batch issued to that unit.

Killed in action on 4 October 1917, Cecil was one of the men lost by the battalion on the first day of the Battle of Broodseinde. Though, again, it cannot be ascertained whether he was a casualty of the initial assault or fell later in the day.

It was Cecil's father who received his savings of £3.4/11d and a war gratuity of £6.00. His mother was initially in receipt of a dependant's pension of 5/- a week. However, when she died in June 1932, the benefit passed to Cecil's father, Edgar, who survived his wife by only two years, passing away in June 1934.

Cecil's brother, Edwin, also enlisted in 1916 and initially as Private 73866 Postle, he served in the RE and qualified as a signaller. He was attached to 92 Brigade of the RGA. Discharged in 1919, Edwin lived in Norwich until his death in 1960.

As Cecil has no known grave, he is commemorated on the memorial wall of Tyne Cot Cemetery. He is also commemorated in his home village of Newton Flotman, where his name is recorded on a wooden plaque installed in the village church of St Mary the Virgin. The plaque also records the names of a further seventeen men from the area who fell in the Great War.

Thomas Edgar Revell – Private 300272

Killed in action on 4 October 1917, aged 24 years.
Commemorated at Tyne Cot Memorial.
Panel 27.

Located just a couple of miles inland from the northern coast of the county of Kent lies the small village of Chislet. It was here, in the third quarter of 1884, that Thomas Revell was born to Thomas, a nursery labourer, and his wife, Matilda. He was baptised on 4 November of that year, at Dover.

The family home was located on the Canterbury Road and it was here, in 1900, that the couple's second child, Ethel, was born. She was followed by Rose, though there was a significant gap between the daughters, given that the 1911 Census records her as being just one month old. Strangely, the census also records that of three children born to the couple, only two had survived. Yet the survey clearly shows that all three of the aforementioned children are alive.

By 1911, the family had moved from Chislet and were living in a six-roomed house at 46, Mortimer Street, Herne Bay. Thomas Snr was not working by this time and instead is shown as living by 'private means', perhaps suggesting that he had received an inheritance that enabled him to retire. Young Thomas was by then 15 and working as a journeyman butcher.

Given that Thomas's service record no longer exists, only basic information can be gleaned about his service. It is possible to say that he enlisted at Canterbury, around February 1915. His unit was The Buffs and he was initially given the service number of 4554. Though there is no information available to confirm exactly when he entered the Western Front theatre, it is possible to say that he was still with The Buffs in early 1917. This is because new service numbers were issued to the territorial infantry at that time and Thomas received the new service number 201597. From this, it can initially be established that he was with the 4th Bn, The Buffs. This can be narrowed down further to the 2/4, a second line unit that remained in England throughout the war. The unit was raised in Canterbury in September 1914 and is most likely to be the unit that Thomas originally enlisted with.

At some unknown point after renumbering, Thomas has then been shipped over to France and transferred to the strength of the 1/7 Royal Warwicks. He subsequently fell in battle on 4 October 1917, aged 24 years.

Thomas nominated his mother, Matilda, as his sole beneficiary. As such, she received his savings of £2.9/1d and a war gratuity of £7.00. Pension records also confirm that Matilda was the recipient of a dependant's pension. However, the amount she received is not recorded, though it would probably have been a basic pension of 5/- a week. According to probate records for 1918, Thomas also bequeathed the sum of £119.11/- to Matilda. At the time he drafted his will, his address was given as the Bijou Picture House, High Street in Herne Bay. Though surviving as a cinema up to the late 1930s, his former home later saw use as a clothing factory and then conversion to retail use. The building is still in use today and retains much of its original facade.

As one of the missing, Thomas is commemorated on the memorial wall at Tyne Cot Cemetery. However, his name is not recorded on either the memorial plaque in Chislet parish church, or on the main war memorial at Herne Bay. It is therefore unknown at this time whether he is locally commemorated elsewhere.

Henry Frederick Rodgers – 2nd Lieutenant

Died on 4 October 1917, aged 24 years.
Commemorated at Tyne Cot Memorial.
Panel 23.

Little is known about the early life of Henry Rodgers, save to say that he was born in Australia in 1893 and was the son of a solicitor, William Alexander Rodgers, and his wife, Georgina. He is also known to have had a sister, Winifred, who was around six years his senior.

By the time of the 1915 Australian Census, Henry is recorded as living at 18, the Esplanade, in Perth, Western Australia. His occupation is listed as an accountant and his age as 22 years. Though, what happened later in that year would trigger a sequence of events that would not only see Henry travel halfway across the world to do his bit, but also demonstrate his singular determination to make that happen.

On 4 November, Henry went to the central recruiting office in Perth with the intention of joining the Australian Imperial Force (AIF). However, things did not go to plan and after a medical examination his application was rejected due to 'defective sight'. No doubt realising that the situation was hopeless in his homeland, he then took the extraordinary decision to travel to England and attempt to enlist there.

Henry's sister, Winifred, was already living in England, having married a jute merchant by the name of Laurence Woods in 1909. It seems that Henry did not delay in taking passage to England and arrived soon after his rejection by the AIF. By that time, his sister and her husband were living at 53, Drewstead Road in Streatham Hill, southwest London. Henry's service records confirm that this was the address he gave on enlistment.

The next part of Henry's plan took place on 13 January 1916 when he took the military oath in London and was accepted for service as Airman 18020 Rodgers of the Royal Flying Corps (RFC). Henry's medical form describes him as being 23 years old, standing 5' 9¼" tall, with a 34½" chest and with a 2½" expansion. He listed Winfred as his next of kin.

Henry joined his unit at South Farnborough the next day and on 19 March, he was posted to France where he was promoted to Airman 1st Class on 1 July 1916. Though it appears that Henry had achieved his wish to serve, it seems that he wanted to see more action than his RFC duties offered. Having returned to England on 1 February 1917, he took steps to ensure that he would experience service in the front line and obtained attachments to the 1st and 2nd battalions of the Royal Warwicks. This ultimately led to his discharge from the RFC on 26 June, 1917, having received a regular army emergency commission. His subsequent attachment to the 1/7 Royal Warwicks as 2nd Lieutenant Rodgers soon followed.

On the morning of 4 October 1917, Henry led his platoon into battle and was likely killed in the initial assault wave as German machine gunners fiercely defended their positions, taking a heavy toll of both officers and men. Though unlike the death of Captain John Croall, no contemporary accounts or letters that explain what happened to him have so far been located.

Henry left effects totalling £82.11/10d that he left to his sister, Winifred, and brother-in-law, Laurance Woods. The civil probate record for London, 9 November 1917, also records that he left a further bequest of the remainder of his estate, again to Laurance and Winifred, of £318.12/6d.

Henry's remains have no known resting place and he is therefore commemorated at Tyne Cot on the memorial wall. It is not known if he is commemorated on any memorials, either in England or his native Australia, though his name is recorded at the Australian National War Memorial.

Bertram Thomas Rowe – Private 266599

Missing in action, presumed dead on 8 October 1917, aged 21 years.
Commemorated at Tyne Cot Memorial.
Panel 27.

Bertram Rowe was born in the parish of Holy Trinity, Coventry, on 27 August 1896. The parish baptism records for that year confirm that he was christened on 11 November 1896 and was the son of Charles, then working as a machinist, and Ada (nee Carter). Home for the family was 24, New Buildings in the city centre.

In the coming years, Bertram was followed by the birth of two brothers: Frederick, born on 3 July 1898, and Leonard, born on 23 June 1899. However, neither boy survived their first year, with Frederick dying just seven days after his birth and Leonard passing away just a little over a month after his birth, on 1 August.

By the time of the 1901 Census, the family were still resident at the New Buildings address and Charles was working as an enameller in the cycle manufacturing trade. Later that year Bertram gained a sister, with the birth of Edith on 7 October. Two further children would follow. Hilda, born on 8 July 1906, and Ernest, who arrived on 10 April 1909.

Private Bertram Rowe. Note the Imperial Service Badge worn on the right breast. (*Public domain*)

The 1911 Census again records the family address as New Buildings and Charles had changed his occupation once more, this time working for the local corporation as a storekeeper. Bertram too, at 14 years old, was also in employment and working as a lithograph printer. The following year, on 7 July, another child, Winifred, was born.

On 20 October 1915, Bertram's youngest sibling, Sidney, was also born. His birth came just one day after Bertram had enlisted with the 1/7 Royal Warwicks at Coventry as Private 4509 Rowe. His address at the time was given as 1, Pridmore Road, in the Foleshill area of Coventry.

Signing on for the duration of the war, Bertram also signed Army Form E.624, the waiver that allowed him as a territorial to be posted for duty overseas. In doing so, he was entitled to wear the Imperial Service badge, which he can be seen wearing in his photo.

After basic training in England, Bertram landed in France on 7 March 1916. From there, on 19 March, he joined his battalion that, at that time, were holding front-line trenches close to the villages of Fonquevillers and Souastre. On 22 June, the battalion was moved into trenches in G Sector at Hebuterne. There, on 1 July 1916, they witnessed the sustained British artillery bombardment that preceded the opening assault on the first day of the Battle of the Somme.

As ordered, the battalion held the trenches in G Sector, while the attacking infantry units moved forward to take their objectives, at heavy cost. Subjected to heavy shelling from the enemy, the battalion also sustained several casualties that day. Intermittent German shelling continued the following day and this was when Bertram was evacuated from the field by the 1/2 SMFA, suffering from shell shock. From there, he went via 19 CCS to a convalescent depot at Le Havre and was admitted with a 'light' case of shell shock on 4 July.

Sufficiently recovered to return to duty, Bertram was sent to Rouen on 12 July and then briefly joined the 1/8 Royal Warwicks on the twenty-eighth of that month. However, by 7 August, he had rejoined the 1/7 Royal Warwicks, which were then engaged in training near the town of Mesnil-Domquer.

Bertram required further medical treatment on 30 December 1916, when he fell ill with a fever. The SMFA evacuated him from a training camp near Albert. From there, he was sent to the Divisional Rest Station (DRS), though the record does not state for how long. His service record also shows that he was granted ten days' days leave on 25 August 1917. Though this was taken 'in the field', so he did not have the opportunity to return home.

Bertram was initially reported as wounded in action on 8 October and later as missing, presumed killed. His father, Charles, received Bertram's savings of £2.9/11d and a war gratuity of £9.00. His mother, Ada, was awarded a dependant's pension of 5/- a week.

As one of the missing, Bertram's name is commemorated on the memorial wall at Tyne Cot Cemetery. He is also commemorated on the Coventry Roll of Honour and remembered at the city's War Memorial Park.

Thomas Henry Scott – Private (C Coy) 268843

Killed in action on 8 October 1917, aged 23 years.
Buried at Cement House Cemetery.
Grave reference: X. E. 31.

Inscription reads:

DEAREST AND BEST WE SHALL MEET
AGAIN WITH GOD, THE REST

Born in Bromyard, Hereford in the first quarter of 1894, Thomas Scott was the oldest child of Henry Scott, a railway worker, and Louisa (nee Gardener).

In the years following Thomas's birth, the couple had a further two children, Gladys and Harold, who, at the time of the 1901 census, were aged three and two, respectively. Home for the family at this time was in Worcester, though unfortunately, the address recorded on the census form is illegible. However, given the occupations listed for their neighbours, it can be seen that the area they lived in was very much working-class. Many of the local men are listed as either working in manufacturing, engineering or on the railways.

Tragedy befell the young family in March 1907 when, at 40 years old, Henry died. From that point, life would change dramatically for his children. Especially as the following month, Louisa would have an extra mouth to feed when she gave birth to the last of Henry's children, Evelyn.

With no husband to support her at the time, the available records indicate that Louisa placed her three eldest children into care. Though it is not known at what point she did this, Thomas, Harold and Gladys all appear on the records as pupils at The Railway Orphanage, located on the Ashbourne Road in Derby. Entry to the orphanage at that time was granted only to those children whose parent or parents had died while in service on the railways. It can therefore be assumed that Henry was killed in an accident at work.

In the spring of 1909, Louisa remarried to Albert Mealings, a railway goods guard. They set up home at 7, Midland Road, Worcester and by the time of the 1911 Census, Louisa had given Albert a daughter. This was Ethel, who was just 11 months old at the time of the survey. Interestingly, though the orphanage census records show Thomas, Gladys and Harold as still being resident there, the record for the Mealings household also shows not only Evelyn present at Midland Road, but Thomas too. Presumably he had only recently left the orphanage after completion of their census return and was then living with his mother and stepfather. Crucially, the 17-year-old was now capable of earning a living and had started work as a porter on the railways. His income was no doubt a welcome addition to the household coffers.

By the time of his enlistment, on 11 December 1915, Thomas was working for the Great Western Railway company as a district lampman. He enlisted at Worcester into the 7th Bn Royal Warwicks as Private 4297 Scott and his service record describes him as being 5′ 6½″ tall, with a 38″ chest, having a 4″ expansion. At the time, he was 21 years old, weighed 147lbs and was of good physical development.

Once enlisted, Thomas remained in England in the battalion reserve, awaiting mobilisation. It was late on in this waiting period that his younger brother, Harold, also enlisted at Worcester. He joined up some time after April 1917, initially in the Hampshire Regiment as Private 42807 Scott. Though, he later transferred to the 6th Bn, the Duke of Edinburgh's (Wiltshire) Regiment and was issued with a new service number, 27915.

Thomas was subsequently mobilised in the April of 1917 and sailed from Southampton on 3 August. He initially joined the Infantry Base Depot (IBD) at Rouen, before transferring back to the Royal Warwicks, joining the 1/7 in the field on 29 August. At the time, the battalion was completing Lewis Gun and musketry training at Sint-Jan ter-Biezen, prior to operational deployment the following day in the Ypres sector.

Thomas survived the fighting over the three-day period of the Battle of Broodseinde. However, his service record states that he was wounded in action on 8 October and subsequently died from his wounds. This being the day after the battalion was relieved in the field. The fact that his body received a proper burial at Cement House Cemetery bears out that he was likely evacuated to a nearby aid post or CCS, before succumbing to his wounds. The cemetery was in active use at the time, conducting burials for battlefield casualties. Thomas, if not lying in his original grave, therefore now lies very close to his original burial spot.

His mother, Louisa, would subsequently receive his savings of £2.11/18d, along with a war gratuity of £3.00. However, Louisa's grief over the loss of her eldest son would soon be compounded by the death of her youngest, Harold. He was killed just six months later, on 10 April 1918. Ironically, this was during the fighting to retain the ground taken during the battle that killed his brother. This was when the German army launched its Spring Offensive and subsequently reversed all of the territorial gains made by the British and Imperial forces. Harold was 19 years old when he died.

Though Thomas lies in Cement House Cemetery, Louisa was denied the small comfort of knowing that her youngest son also had a final resting place as his body was never recovered from the battlefield. Harold is therefore remembered at Tyne Cot Cemetery on the memorial wall to the missing.

Pension records exist for the Scott brothers and list Louisa as the beneficiary for both. However, no award amounts are recorded. Records also show that Harold left his mother savings of £2.19/3d. She also received a further war gratuity payment of £3.00.

It is not known if either Thomas or Harold are commemorated locally on any civic memorials. However, their names are remembered on the gravestone of their father, Henry, who rests in Astwood Cemetery, Worcester.

James Ernest Shergold – Private 203568

Killed in action on 4 October 1917, aged 20 years.
Commemorated at Tyne Cot Memorial.
Panel 27A.

Very little information exists in relation to James Shergold. Records confirm that he was the fourth child of iron and steel stamper Arthur Shergold and his wife, Rose (nee Sanders). Birth records indicate that he was born in the third quarter of 1897 in the Aston district of Birmingham, close to the city's industrial and manufacturing heart.

The 1901 Census records that the family lived in the back of 35, Sandy Lane, Aston, in what would have been very cramped accommodation for such a growing and already quite large family, totalling eight people.

It is believed that, somewhere between 1901 and 1903, the Shergolds left Birmingham and made a new home in Coventry. The first official mention of their residence in the city is in the 1911 Census, when the family is recorded as living in the back of 438, Stoney Stanton Road. Though the building itself no longer exists, it was situated within a highly industrialised area. As with their previous home in Aston, the house itself would have been extremely cramped, amounting to little more than three bedrooms and a sitting room, to house a family that had swelled to twelve, comprising five boys, five girls and their parents.

The census record also reveals that, during the course of their marriage, the couple had three other children, who had not survived. Of those who did survive, their names and ages are recorded that year, as follows: Frederick, 18, Louisa, 16, Arthur, 15, James, 12, Albert, 11, Annie, 9, Charles, 7, Florence, 4, Nellie, 3, and finally Beatrice at just 18 months old.

While it is known that James enlisted at Coventry, the date is uncertain and can only be estimated from the war gratuity paid to his family as in the year following October 1916. However, given the lack of surviving records, other than the date of his death, nothing further is known about his military service. James was killed in action on 4 October 1917, the first day of the Battle of Broodseinde, and his body was never recovered for burial.

It is thought that, at the time of his death, or shortly after, James's parents had moved to 78, Uplands in the Stoke Heath area of Coventry. His father, Arthur, received payment of a war gratuity of £3.00 and received his son's savings of £2.2/8d. His mother, Rose, was awarded a dependant's pension of 5/- a week. However, Rose passed away in October of 1919 and the relevant pension records do not record either her death, which is unusual, or whether the pension then became payable to Arthur, which is normally the case.

As one of the missing, James is commemorated at the Tyne Cot memorial. It is not known if he is commemorated locally.

Frederick Simpson – Private 266371

Killed in action on 8 October 1917, age unknown.
Commemorated at Tyne Cot Memorial.
Panel 27A.

Despite exhaustive enquiries across numerous databases, no information was uncovered that could connect Frederick Simpson to a known historical individual. Under normal circumstances, a picture of an individual can be formed by cross-referencing numerous different types of records. These span records held by the CWGC, genealogical sources such as birth and census information, and military records such as surviving service records, medal awards and effects information. However, in the case of Frederick, no links could be made between the various sources to identify a definite match to this fallen serviceman.

There were records available from the Coventry area that provided possibilities. However, because vital information was missing from other sources, the cross-checking of data, needed to positively identify that person, was not possible. Consequently, what information does exist is extremely basic.

The only certain facts we have about Frederick is that he enlisted with the 1/7 Royal Warwicks at Coventry, around January 1915, and was originally issued with the service number 3948. Frederick is then recorded on his medal index card as landing in France on 27 June 1915. Thereby entitling him to the award of the 1914-15 Star.

At the time that Frederick joined his battalion, they were billeted in the Lozinghem area, undergoing training and refitting before deploying to front-line trenches at Hebuterne, late the following month.

Frederick was killed in action in the Ypres sector on 8 October 1917 and his body was not recovered for burial. He is therefore commemorated on the memorial wall at Tyne Cot Cemetery.

Frustratingly, no pension records exist for Frederick and the only clue as to his family background is within his record of effects. Here, it is recorded that his sister, Elizabeth B Hunt, received his savings of £6.18/6d and a war gratuity payment of £12.10/-. Elizabeth was recorded as Frederick's sole legatee and despite an extensive search of civil archives, no records of her have been uncovered.

Frederick Henry South – Private 266091

Killed in action on 4 October 1917, aged 23 years.
Commemorated at Tyne Cot Memorial.
Panel 27.

Frederick South was born in Stratford-upon-Avon, Warwickshire in July 1894. He was the second child of Henry and Eliza (nee Edwards).

In the 1901 Census, the family are recorded as living at 23, Shakespeare Street, in the town. This was a modest, four-roomed, terraced house that still stands today. As well as six-year-old Frederick and his parents, the family consisted of his eldest sister, Ada, who was then eight, and younger brothers Ernest, three, and William, one.

By the time of the 1911 Census, the family were still resident at 23, Shakespeare Street, but had grown by a further two children, Edgar, seven, and one year old, Edith. Henry was by then working as a maltsters labourer and Frederick, by then 16, had started work as a brewery labourer. The oldest child, Ada, had found work as a domestic servant, while the rest of the South children were at school.

By the time Frederick enlisted at Stratford-upon-Avon, on 16 November 1914, the family had moved to a new address in the town, 17, Percy Street. A similar property to their old house and again, one that still stands today.

Having been accepted for service in the 7th Bn Royal Warwicks, Frederick was initially issued with the service number 3397 and embodied into his unit on the same day. He was then sent to commence basic training. Upon completion, Frederick was shipped to France and initially reported to the Infantry Base Depot (IBD) at Harfleur on 26 July 1915. By late September he had been transferred to his battalion in the field, but by Boxing Day of that year, he had to be evacuated by 1/1 SMFA, while suffering from scabies. This was a very common disease, arising from the unsanitary conditions endured by troops in the trenches. The condition kept him out of the field for just over a month before he returned to the battalion.

Frederick was again admitted to hospital the following February, suffering from an inflammation of connective tissue in his right foot. This again kept him off the front line, this time for about five days, before he again returned to duty.

On 14 July 1916, Frederick's unit moved into trenches close to La Boiselle. Whilst moving into the positions the battalion had been heavily shelled, but still commenced an assault on fiercely defended German positions. The action left 52 men dead and around twice that number wounded. Frederick sustained a gunshot wound to his right arm during this action and was evacuated from the front line by field ambulance. Initially, he was taken to No.34 CCS at Vecquemont, but was then transferred to No.11 General Hospital at Rouen, before moving to Etaples for further treatment and recovery.

Once fit to resume his duties, Frederick arrived at 29 IBD at Rouen on 11 August. He subsequently returned to his battalion on the twenty-seventh of that month. At the time, the unit was engaged in operations, based in trenches close to Ovillers.

In terms of Frederick's movements overall, his service record is incomplete. Therefore, while it can be seen that at some stage after his return to duty he returned to England, there is no record to confirm either when or why this happened. The only certain information is that he returned to the strength of the BEF on 14 April 1917.

Once back at the front, Frederick suffered further medical issues and was again evacuated for medical treatment to 9 CCS at Aveluy for what appears to be a dental issue. From there, he was once again sent to 29 IBD at Rouen before again rejoining his battalion in training at Bienvillers on 15 July.

Frederick South was subsequently killed in action on 4 October 1917 – the first day of the battle of Broodseinde. Nominated as his sole beneficiary, his mother, Eliza, received his savings of £6.12/2d and payment of a war gratuity of £13.10/-. She was also awarded a dependant's pension of 6/- a week.

As Frederick's body was never found, he is commemorated on the memorial wall at Tyne Cot Cemetery. He is also remembered locally on the Stratford-upon-Avon war memorial cross. Originally located in Bridge Street, the monument now stands in the town's garden of remembrance, located at the junction of Old Town and College Street.

Cecil Edward Stone – Private 265101

Killed in action on 5 October 1917, aged 23 years.
Buried at Dozinghem Military Cemetery.
Grave reference: V. G. 15.

By the time Cecil Stone was born in the last quarter of 1894, the Stone family was already on the way to being quite large. His father, William, a gardener, and mother, Anna Marie, had started their family in the Norwich area and already had Edna, Christopher, Lily and Bertie. Of those eldest children, the first three had been born in Norwich but the last, Bertie, had been born in Southam, Warwickshire. This indicates that the family had moved from the county of Norfolk to Warwickshire, sometime between 1891 and 1893.

The 1901 Census has the family living at 1, Duke Street, in Leamington Spa. Though, given that records confirm Cecil was born in nearby Southam, Warwickshire, the family may have only recently moved into the town. Cecil, by then six years old, had also acquired two younger brothers by that time, John and Edward, who were four and two respectively.

By the time of the 1911 Census, the family had moved again. This time to 12, Chandos Street, in the town centre. The family had also grown again, by a further four children: William, Frederick, Evelyn and Reginald, the youngest, at three years old.

By this time, Cecil was 16 and working as a printer. Christopher, his eldest brother, had joined the Regular Army and was now Private 1758 Stone of the 2nd Bn Royal Warwicks, based at Budbrooke Barracks, Warwickshire. Other than Christopher, this meant that the remaining twelve people in the Stone family were crammed into a house comprising of just five rooms.

With the coming of war, Christopher remained in the army and was in France by 4 October 1914. It appears that Cecil's next oldest brother, Bertie, had also enlisted in the regular army at Warwick and likely before the outbreak of war, joined the 1st Bn, Seaforth Highlanders (The Seaforths). Records confirm that he was serving with the unit when it landed in France in October of 1914. Prior to their deployment in France, the battalion was stationed in India.

As for Cecil, though his service record has not survived, there is sufficient documentation available to establish that, at the very outbreak of war, he enlisted at Leamington, joining the 1/7 Royal Warwicks as Private 1488 Stone. He subsequently entered the Western Front theatre of war with the rest of his battalion on 22 March 1915. Thereby being with them right at the very start of their participation in the war.

On 6 June 1915, Cecil was with his unit, in front-line trenches at Wulverghem, in Belgium. His brother, Bertie, was with his unit, back across the border in France, in the area of Lestrem and Richebourg, around twenty miles away. The weather in that part of France had been hot for some days and the men of 1 Seaforths had taken to routinely bathing in the canal at Lestrem. It was during one such bathing session that Bertie tragically drowned in the canal. Corporal Bertie Stone was around 22 years old when he was laid to rest at Cabaret-Rouge British Cemetery, Souchez, Pas de Calais, France. (Grave reference XVII.D.15.)

The following year, both Cecil's and his older brother, Christopher's, battalions were involved in the ongoing Battle of the Somme. On 3 September Christopher's unit, 2nd Bn Royal Warwicks, was involved in a battalion assault on enemy positions around the Pommiers Redoubt, close to the village of

Leamington Spa town war memorial. (*Author's photo*)

Ginchy. Although the attack achieved many of its objectives, the battalion suffered heavy casualties. Their war diary notes around 129 men across all ranks as either killed or missing, with a further 203 men wounded. Private Christopher Stone was one of the missing and, at 29 years old, was later presumed dead. He is remembered on Pier 9 of the Thiepval Memorial to the missing of the Somme.

At the time of Christopher's death, Cecil was undergoing battle training at Bois de Warnemont, France. It is impossible to know what he felt, both then and in the months that followed, knowing that both of his older brothers had fallen in battle. But he continued to do his duty, eventually participating in his own battalion's attack at the Battle of Broodseinde, where he was fatally wounded. Whether he was wounded on 4 or 5 October is not known, but the existing records confirm that he died on the fifth, at one of the three CCSs based behind the lines, north of the town of Poperinghe.

Cecil's mother, Anna Maria, received his savings of £25.8/11d and a war gratuity payment of £14.10. She also received Bertie's savings of £19.15/6d and a gratuity of £6.00. Christopher nominated his father, William, to receive his savings of £10.11/13d and a gratuity of £11.10/-. Although pension records exist for the brothers, no record is available of any payments awarded.

Cecil was laid to rest at Dozinghem Military Cemetery, which received those soldiers who died while being treated at the 4th, 47th and 61st CCSs. He is also commemorated locally, along with Christopher and Bertie, on the town war memorial located at Euston Place, Leamington Spa.

Herbert Edward Stone – Private 29283

Killed in action on 8 October 1917, aged 28 years.
Buried at Tyne Cot Cemetery.
Grave reference: XIII. D. 31.

Inscription reads:

NOT LOST BUT GONE BEFORE

Herbert Stone was born in the village of Earl Soham in the county of Suffolk in the second quarter of 1889. Born into a typical Suffolk farming community, home for Herbert was Street Farm in the village of Great Glemham. This was close to the market town of Saxmundham, in East Suffolk. His father, Henry, was employed as a farm bailiff by the farmer and owner, John Abbott.

The 1891 Census records that Henry's wife, Louisa (nee Clarke), had already borne him three children, Edith, Ellen and Henry, by the time Herbert was born. By the time of the 1901 Census, two further children, Gertrude and Ernest, had also been born by then, with Ernest being the youngest at two years old. However, in June of the same year, Henry passed away at the relatively early age of 43.

The 1911 Census records that the Stone family remained at Street Farm, with Louisa, now as head of the family, continuing to work as a housekeeper. By then only Harry (previously known as Henry), Herbert and Ernest were still living at home, with both Harry and Herbert being 23 and 21 respectively, and both working as cowmen at the farm.

In the early part of 1915, Herbert married Florence May Mouser and the couple set up home in the nearby village of Sweffling. The following year, around October to November, Herbert enlisted at Ipswich with The Norfolks as Private 27409 Stone. His younger brother, Ernest, was also keen to do his bit and he too enlisted at Ipswich in the month after his brother, then being accepted for service in the King's Royal Rifle Corps (KRRC). However, although he was initially posted to the 22nd Training Reserve as Rifleman TR/10/7633, it is likely he lied about his age, given that he was only 17 at the time. Nevertheless, Ernest went on to serve with the 8th Bn, KRRC.

Herbert's service record no longer exists and there is therefore no information available to shed light on his time in the army. Although, given that he retained a five-figure service number, it is unlikely that he was with a TF battalion at the time they were renumbered in 1917. Rather that he was still with one of the battalions raised as part of Kitchener's Army, at least until later into 1917.

Herbert was reported as being killed in action on 8 October 1917 and may have received a field burial in one of the many makeshift cemeteries that sprung up across the front. His remains were found after the war, when recovery teams were exhuming the dead and reburying them in larger cemeteries. He was identified by a book and letter he was carrying at the time he died and was subsequently laid to rest at Tyne Cot Cemetery.

In the March following Herbert's death, the 8th Bn KRRC were in trenches close to the village of Urvillers, France. On the twenty-ninth, during heavy fighting and a subsequent German counter-attack that surrounded their positions, the battalion suffered heavy casualties. At 18 years old, Rifleman A/205401 Ernest Stone was one of the men killed in action that day.

Initially, Ernest was originally buried at St Benoite German Military Cemetery. Though after the war, his remains were also exhumed and reburied at St Souplet British Cemetery. (Grave ref: I.G.4.353.)

Herbert's widow, Florence, received her husband's savings of £3.3/1d and a war gratuity of £3.00. She was also awarded a dependant's pension of 13/9d a week. Louisa received a £5.00 war gratuity in respect of her son, Ernest. She also received his savings of £6.16/5d. The records do not reflect if she received a dependant's pension, although Ernest is mentioned on pension record cards.

As well as their respective graves, the Stone brothers are commemorated locally. Herbert's name is included on a memorial plaque inside St Mary the Virgin Parish Church in Sweffling and Ernest is commemorated on the war memorial cross located in the churchyard of All Saints parish church, Great Glemham.

Albert Edward Swann – Private 34011

Killed in action on 4 October 1917, aged 28 years.
Commemorated at Tyne Cot Memorial.
Panel 27.

Lying close to the county border with Cambridgeshire, Hadstock is a village in rural North Essex. It was here in the last quarter of 1889 that Albert Swann was born. He was the son of Arthur, an agricultural labourer, and Sarah (nee Malyon).

The 1891 Census records that the Swanns already had five children before the arrival of Albert. Moreover, the extended family in the village amounted to a total of fifteen Swanns living in three properties on Walden Road, which was the main route through the village. All of the men of the family were engaged in agricultural work.

By the time of the 1901 Census, the family had grown with the addition of Clara, who was then seven years old. Albert, by then 11 years old, was already employed as an agricultural labourer, along with his older brothers, Horace, who was 17, and George, aged 14.

Albert would subsequently move out of his family's traditional work in agriculture and the 1911 Census records him as working as a carman, which was somebody who transported goods. Home was then 24, Langley Road, Luton, Bedfordshire. A five-roomed house where he was a boarder under the roof of Robert and Emma Rutland and their eight-year-old daughter, Violet. Boarding there too was 23-year-old William Bradshaw, also a carman.

Though records could not be located to confirm the full details, Albert married soon after the census to a girl called Beatrice, more commonly known as Bertie. By January of 1913, their first child, Norman, was born and he was followed in March of the following year by Aubrey. Home for the couple at the time is believed to initially have been 89, Warwick Road, Luton, a small end-of-terrace property that still stands today. It seems though that Albert was keen to return to rural Essex and soon took his new family back to his home village, there to take up residence at Hill Farm.

Due to the absence of service records, it is only possible to say that Albert enlisted sometime after October 1916. This took place in Luton and he subsequently became Private 202635 of the 4th Bn, The Buffs. It is not known when he was transferred to the 1/7 Royal Warwicks but pension records confirm that he was in C Coy, 11 Platoon at the time he was killed in action on 4 October 1917. His Company, commanded by Captain John Croall, were first into the attack that day, along with D Coy. Though it is impossible to say whether Albert was killed at the opening of the attack, C Coy took the brunt of the German response. They were raked with machine gun fire at the outset, killing and injuring many of the men in the opening minutes of the assault. If Albert had survived that then he would have only gone on to meet further heavy enemy resistance as they pushed on to take Tweed House, one of the battalion objectives.

Albert's widow, Bertie, later received her husband's savings of £2.9/11d, along with a war gratuity of £3.00. She was also awarded a dependant's pension of 25/5d a week.

As Albert's body was not recovered for burial, he is remembered on the memorial wall at Tyne Cot. He is also commemorated on a small wooden plaque in the parish church of St Botolph's, in his home village of Hadstock.

Percy Swingler – Private 268854

Killed in action on 8 October 1917, aged 28 years.
Commemorated at Tyne Cot Memorial.
Panel 27.

Percy Swingler was born in the village of Stanion, Northamptonshire on 18 November 1888. He was the fourth child of John Swingler, an engine driver, and Mary Ann (nee Gray). The oldest of his siblings was Luther, followed by Sarah, Herbert, then Mabel. After Percy came Lilly, Clara and George. Resident too with the family was Robert Gray, Mary Ann's father and a widower.

The census for 1911 records that Percy's older brothers had started work by then. Nineteen-year-old Luther was a blacksmith and Herbert, 15, was an agricultural labourer. Percy was still at school by that time. But, by the 1911 Census, the then 20-year-old Percy is recorded as boarding at 45, Centaur

Road, Coventry, with Alfred and Ethel Humphries and another boarder, James Kent. Both Percy and James were working as bakers and James too was a Northamptonshire lad, from Wellingborough.

Percy was still living in Coventry when war started and was living at 72, Widdrington Road when, on 11 December 1915, he enlisted at Coventry in the 7th Bn Royal Warwicks. From that point he would remain in the reserves until his mobilisation in 1917.

Percy must have been able to go back to his old home in Stanion from time to time because he eventually met his future wife, Alice Emma Halford. She had previously been a scullery maid in the service of Admiral Michael Culme-Seymour at Wadenhoe House, Wadenhoe, Northamptonshire.

Mobilised on 24 April 1917, Percy was posted to the 7th Bn Royal Warwicks the following day. Perhaps knowing that Percy would not have too much time left at home before being sent to fight, the couple married in the village of Quinton, not far from Stanion, on 5 June 1917. Home for the newlyweds was at 48, Digby Street in Kettering, Northamptonshire. A small, end-of-terrace house, which still stands today.

Inevitably, it was not long before Percy was sent to France and he sailed out of Folkestone, bound for Boulogne, on 3 August. The day after landing, he arrived at 29 IBD at Rouen. From there he joined the 1/7 Royal Warwicks at Tunneling Camp, near the village of Sint-Jan-ter-Biezen, as they underwent reorganisation, followed by a month of battle training.

By 1 October, the battalion had moved to the front and into Dambre Camp, outside Ypres, in preparation for their attack on the fourth. This was Percy's first time in action and he survived that battle, only to go missing in action the day after the battalion had been relieved. He was later presumed dead.

As Percy's widow, Alice was his sole legatee and received his savings of £3.2/5d and a war gratuity of £3.00. She was also awarded a dependant's pension of 13/9d a week.

As well as his inclusion on the memorial to the missing at Tyne Cot, Percy is commemorated on the Northamptonshire town of Corby's Roll of Honour. He is also commemorated on a plaque inside St Peter the Apostle parish church in his home village of Stanion. He is remembered along with two other men from the parish who fell in the Great War.

It appears Alice did not remarry after Percy was killed and initially moved to Hertfordshire. She subsequently emigrated at some stage after this, dying in Bulawayo, Rhodesia on 3 February 1958 at around 66 years of age.

Albert Arthur Thurston – Private 29289

Killed in action on 8 October 1917, aged 19 years.
Commemorated at Tyne Cot Memorial.
Panel 28A.

By the time of his birth, on 6 May 1898, Albert Thurston was the eighth child born to George Thurston, a domestic coachman, and his wife, Marion (nee Randall). In total, the couple had nine children, though only six survived, with five being recorded on the 1911 Census. They were Earnest, a 15-year-old labourer, and 14-year-old Walter, a houseboy. Albert was 12 at the time and along with his younger sisters, Ethel, 10, and Dorothy, seven, was still in school. Brother George, who was around six years older than Albert, had moved out by that time. Home for the family was a four-roomed house on North Road, Ormesby St Margaret, Norfolk. This small village lies close to the seaside town of Great Yarmouth and is the place where all the Thurston children, including Albert, were born.

Of all of the Thurston brothers, evidence of military service could only be located for George and Albert and it appears that both brothers enlisted at around the same time. George enlisted at Great Yarmouth in the year after August 1916 and Albert enlisted from around October 1916 onwards. Initially, George joined the Royal Field Artillery (RFA) as Gunner 146744 Thurston, though he later transferred to the 6th Bn, Royal Irish Regiment (The Royal Irish) as Private 10156.

Albert also enlisted at Great Yarmouth, joining the 7th Bn, the Norfolks as Private 27364 Thurston. As with George's, Albert's service record no longer exists. However, his battalion had been in France since May of 1915 and he is therefore likely to have joined them in the field, soon after completion of his basic training. From that point on, it is impossible to say where he might have served, given that he later received a further and final five-figure service number of 29289, which he retained up to the point he died. This indicates that he had not transferred to a TF battalion until after the renumbering of early 1917.

It is not possible to say where Albert was when he received news of the death of his brother, George. Though it is highly likely that Albert had transferred to the 1/7 Royal Warwicks by then as they were preparing to take up position in front-line trenches in the St Julien Sector. George was killed on 3 August 1917. His battalion was 'up the line' in trenches at Brandhoek, Belgium, which had been subjected to 'instant' shelling all day. Though the battalion war diary does not name any casualties, it does say that there were 'not many'. However,

George was one of the men who were lost that day. He was 26 years old.

Just over two months later, on 8 October, and just a few miles east of where his brother had been killed, Albert also fell.

It appears that neither of the brothers had married as George named his mother, Marion, as his sole legatee. She received his savings of £8.3/11d and a war gratuity of £4.10/-. Albert nominated his father, George, who received his son's savings of £2.12/- and a war gratuity of £3.00. Pension records name both brothers but do not record any awards made.

As neither of the Thurston brothers' bodies were recovered for burial, they are commemorated on separate memorials, close to the battlefields where they fell. George's name

Ormesby St Margaret war memorial. (*Photo credit – Robert Walton, War Memorials Online*)

is engraved on Panel 33 of the Menin Gate Memorial in Ypres. Albert is remembered on the Tyne Cot memorial wall. George and Albert are also commemorated on the grey granite war memorial cross sited not far from where they lived, on North Road, Ormesby St Margaret. George is also listed on the Irish Memorial Record.

Alexander Tod – Corporal 265788

Killed in action on 4 October 1917, aged 19 years.
Commemorated at Tyne Cot Memorial.
Panel 24A.

Alexander Tod was born in Edinburgh, in Midlothian, Scotland, around 1898. He was the second child of Alexander, a tinsmith, and Marjorie (nee Winram). The 1901 Census of Scotland has the family living at 28, Milton Street, Edinburgh. This stone-built terraced house, standing close to the northern edge of Holyrood Park, still stands today. As well as three-year-old Alexander and his parents, his elder sister, Mary, then four, and his one-year-old brother, James, are also recorded as living there.

In the years between the census's, the Tod family grew by a further three children – George, Frank and Marjorie. Although unclear as to when, they also relocated, leaving Scotland and settling in Coventry. The 1911 Census confirms that all of the Tod children had been born in Edinburgh. Therefore, given that young Marjorie was only two at the time of the survey, the family could not have moved down to Coventry before 1909. The family home at the time the census was taken was 141, Harrow Lane and also living with them was Alexander Snr's 30-year-old brother, John, who was also a tinsmith.

Corporal Alexander Tod. (*Photo used by kind permission of Chris Starkey*)

There are no records to say what work young Alexander was engaged in either prior to or at the outbreak of war. Similarly, his service record has not survived. However, he must have signed up very soon after the outbreak of war. Enlisting at Coventry with the 1/7 Royal Warwicks, he was issued with the service number 2895. This, along with war gratuity information, places his enlistment as early as August 1914. Furthermore, it is clear Alexander lied about his age as he could have only been around 16 or 17 at the time he volunteered. Though, it is clear from medal records that he managed to keep his true age a secret as they reveal that he subsequently landed with the battalion in March 1915, when they were first shipped to France.

In September 1915, the battalion was engaged in operations around the Fonquevillers and Bayencourt sectors. This was when Alexander would have received the news that his father had died that month. He would have been around 45 years of age.

Given the fact that Alexander rose to the rank of corporal, it seems that he was deemed a good and reliable soldier, worthy of promotion. Accordingly, on the day of his death, 4 October 1917, he would have been leading a section of men into battle. However, it is impossible to say whether he was one of the many casualties who fell in the opening assault or during the fighting that followed later the same day.

Alexander left his savings of £4.6d to his mother Marjorie. She also received a war gratuity of £15.00 and she was later awarded a dependant's pension of 8/- a week.

As his body was not recovered from the battlefield for burial, Alexander is commemorated on the memorial wall to the missing at Tyne Cot. Although commemorated on the Coventry City Roll of Honour, it is not known if he is included in any local memorials.

James Pressley Tookey – Private 266230

Killed in action on 4 October 1917, aged 36 years.
Commemorated at Tyne Cot Memorial.
Panel 28A.

James Tookey was born in the Lancashire town of Rawtenstall in July 1881. His parents were Alfred and Sarah Jane (nee Whittaker), both of whom worked as weavers in the local cotton mills. Information about James's early life is sketchy, with him next appearing as a nine-year-old in the 1891 Census. At the time, he and his mother were boarding with Fred and Sarah Sunderland and their nine-month-old son, Harold, at 13, Tor View, Haslingden. This being a modest stone cottage that still stands today. However, though Sarah Jane is recorded as still married, Alfred is not shown as resident at the address and has not so far been located on other records for the year.

Though the date is not known, James left Lancashire and settled in Warwickshire. The first evidence of this is a marriage record that shows that James married Jessie Mansell Mary Makepeace at Warwick in October 1903. Their first child, Ethel, was then born at Kenilworth on 17 September 1904. This was followed by the birth of Harold on 21 October 1906. The entry for his baptism on 20 November 1906 records James as being employed as a gardener. On 16 May 1912, James and Jessie saw the birth of their third child, Alice.

An entry in Spennel's Trade Directory for Kenilworth for 1907 also records James as a gardener and resident in Spring Lane, Kenilworth. A subsequent trade directory entry for 1909 reaffirms his trade and address as 26, Spring Road, a modest mid-terrace house. As does the 1911 Census.

With the coming of war, James enlisted at Coventry into the 7th Bn Royal Warwicks. He signed up on 14 December 1914 and although he was still living in

Private James Tookey. (*Public domain*)

Spring Lane, his occupation had since changed. His service records state that he was then working as a factory hand at Courtaulds in Coventry.

James was issued with an initial service number of 3685. His medical exam notes record him as being 33 years and 4 months old and 5′ 3″ tall. He was of good physical development with a 33″ chest and a 3″ expansion.

On 26 May 1915, James sailed for France. He was then posted to the 1st Entrenching Battalion at Harfleurs before eventually joining the 1/7 Royal Warwicks as part of a draft of 25 ORs at Fonquevillers on 19 November. At the time, the battalion was engaged in working parties, having just been relieved from front-line trenches close to the town.

On 17 April 1916, James's battalion once more took over front-line trenches at Fonquevillers. The weather was poor, with more or less constant rain until the twenty-second, when James was evacuated by 1/1 SMFA with influenza. He remained at 48 DRS until 29 April, when he rejoined the battalion at Souastre for field training.

Though it does not say why, James was sent to the Third Army rest camp at St Valery Sur Somme on 10 May 1917, before returning to his unit on 25 May. At the time, they were in training at Velu.

On 3 July, James was sent to Fifth Army training school, becoming batman to Captain John Croall. He was then granted leave from 20 to 30 August, before rejoining his unit once more and taking up his duties with Captain Croall. He was subsequently killed in action on 4 October, reportedly while trying to save Captain Croall, who was also killed that morning during the opening assault.

James's widow, Jessie, received her husband's savings of £2.12/3d and a war gratuity payment of £13.00. She was also awarded a dependant's pension of 26/3d a week.

James's remains were never recovered from the battlefield and as such, he is remembered on the memorial wall to the missing at Tyne Cot Cemetery. He is also commemorated locally, on the war memorial that stands at the top of Abbey Fields, Kenilworth.

William Henry Treadgold – Lance Corporal 266273

Killed in action on 8 October 1917, aged 22 years.
Commemorated at Tyne Cot Memorial.
Panel 24A.

Born in the parish of St Michael's, Coventry in January 1896, William Treadgold was the second child born to metal polisher Henry and his wife,

Annie. His older sister, also Annie, was born two years previously. William was followed two years later by George, who was also born in Coventry. However, at some time after George's birth, the Treadgolds moved to live in London where another daughter, Maud, was born in Fulham, around 1899.

The family appear in the 1901 Census, living at a comfortably sized terraced house at 43, Aslett Street in the Wandsworth area of southwest London. While there, Henry and Annie had two more daughters: Rose, born in 1901, and Hilda, born around 1904.

The family remained resident in London for the 1911 Census. Though, this time, they were recorded as living at 10, Ash Tree Grove, also in Wandsworth. Of the two houses, only the Aslett Street address still remains standing. William by that time was 15 years old and working as an office boy for a house agent.

At some stage between the last census and the outbreak of war, the Treadgold family returned to Coventry and took up residence at 34, Gresham Street, a typical terraced house that still stands and is located close to Ball Hill, in the Stoke area of the city.

At the time of his enlistment at Coventry on 30 December 1914, William was 19 and working as a clerk for the British Thompson Houston Company, a heavy engineering firm based in nearby Raglan Street that produced such things as magnetos, batteries and generators.

William was embodied into the 7th Bn Royal Warwicks that day and was initially allocated the service number of 3762. His medical examination notes record that he stood 5′ 4½″ tall, with a 33″ chest and an expansion of 3 inches. He had fair vision and good physical development. Having completed his basic training, William remained in England in the battalion reserve and it was during that period that his family are believed to have moved again. This time to 6, Meadow Street, in the Spon End area of Coventry.

On 22 May 1916, William was promoted to the rank of lance corporal and sent to France, sailing from Southampton for Le Havre. On 12 July 1916, though it is not clear where or how, William was in the field when he was wounded by shrapnel. Then, on 16 July, having received treatment for his wound, he was sent to 29 IBD at Rouen, before transferring to the 1/7 Royal Warwicks on 30 July. At the time, the battalion was in training at Mesnil.

William remained with his battalion until 15 February 1917, when he was posted to III Corps Light Railway Operating Coy to take up duties as a train guard. However, he subsequently returned to his former unit on 23 May 1917, when they were again in training, this time at Velu.

After a further minor medical issue in July, William was granted a period of ten days' leave, starting on 10 September 1917. He returned to his unit in

British Thompson Houston memorial, Rugby. (*Author's photo*)

time to become involved in preparations for the planned battalion action of 4 October, which he survived, only to be reported missing, presumed dead on 8 October.

William nominated his mother, Annie, as his sole legatee and she received her son's savings of £4.8/11d and a war gratuity of £13.00. She was also awarded a dependant's pension of 7/- a week.

As one of the missing, William is commemorated on the memorial wall at Tyne Cot. However, when research was conducted into local war memorials, it was found that William's name was not included on either of the relevant memorials. Although British Thompson Houston had commissioned a large stone cross at their main site in Rugby and provided a smaller bronze plaque for Coventry workers lost in the war, William's name had not been included on either.

Consequently, as a result of the research carried out into William's story for this book, it was possible with the assistance of Rugby Borough Council, Royal Warwickshire Regiment archives and the Ministry of Defence to set matters right. In 2020, William's name was added to the war memorial cross erected to the memory of those company employees who died in the Great War. The cross was designed by Sir Edwin Lutyens, who also designed the Cenotaph, standing in Whitehall, London. Made of white Portland Stone, and standing 25' (7.5m) high, the British Thompson Houston cross was erected in 1921. Though, having since been moved from its original site, it now stands on Technology Drive, Rugby, just in front of what was the company's main site.

William Treadgold's name, freshly engraved on the British Thompson Houston memorial, Rugby. (*Author's photo*)

William Joseph Wagstaffe DCM – Sergeant 265374

Died on 4 October 1917, aged 24 years.
Commemorated at Tyne Cot Memorial.
Panel 24.

At the time of William Wagstaffe's birth, on 14 March 1893, his father, Joseph, was the licensee of the Butcher's Inn, a pub that is still serving today and located in the small village of Priors Hardwick, southeast Warwickshire. He and his wife, Ann (nee Haynes), had already had three daughters, though only two, Edith and Gertrude, survived, with Emily passing away around three years after William was born.

William's birth was followed by that of brother, Charles, around two years later, and he was the last of the Wagstaffe children to be born in Priors Hardwick. The next child, Horace, was born in Hanslope, Buckinghamshire, around 1897, which was just before the family moved to the Northamptonshire village of Weedon. Here, Joseph found work as a labourer in the Royal Ordnance Depot, located in the village. A further son, Harold, was born around 1899, at Weedon. He was followed by Sophie, Sidney and Constance, who were also born in Weedon.

By the time of the 1911 Census, the family had moved to the Warwickshire town of Nuneaton and were living at Tunnel Cottage, Gadsby Street, in the Attleborough area of the town. Joseph was labouring in one of the local coal mines at the time and William, now 18, was also working down the mine as a clipper. However, by May of that year, he had also enlisted at Nuneaton with the TF.

With the coming of war, William was mobilised on 4 August 1914 and according to De Ruvigny's Roll of Honour, he was subsequently wounded twice while serving in the Somme sector, the first time being on the opening day of the Battle of the Somme on 1 July 1916.

Sergeant William Wagstaff DCM. (*Public domain*)

William was a recipient of the Distinguished Conduct Medal (DCM) and though the date is uncertain, De Ruvigny's also suggest that he was awarded the medal for his actions on 6 April 1917. At the time, the battalion was in action around the village of Epehy, in the Somme sector. The battalion war diary seems to corroborate the date as it describes patrols being sent out between 5 and 7 April, with fighting occurring each time with German forces. The actual citation for William's award is reproduced below and does seem to broadly accord with what the diary says.

The Distinguished Conduct Medal. (*Author's Photo*)

For conspicuous gallantry and devotion to duty. When on patrol a party of the enemy attempted to surround them, he, by good management and coolness, drove off the enemy and succeeded in getting two badly wounded men back a distance of 1,200 yards. He set a fine example of courage and determination.

William was later killed in action during the assault on Terrier Farm on 4 October 1917. He is reported to have been buried where he fell and the location of his grave was subsequently lost. As a clearly well-respected soldier, his commanding officer, Captain Mitford, wrote of him:

Serjt. Wagstaff was a great friend of mine, and was most popular amongst his men. His courage and bravery knew no equal, and we were most sorry when he was killed. We have lost a very great friend.

William nominated both of his parents as joint legatees and they received his savings of £22.3/4d. A war gratuity payment of £17.00 was also made. However, no pension records have so far been located.

As one of the missing, William is commemorated on the memorial wall at Tyne Cot. He is also commemorated locally on a brass memorial plaque situated inside Attleborough Baptist Church, Nuneaton.

John Caleb Wellard – Private 34000

Died of wounds on 8 October 1917, aged 25 years.
Commemorated at Tyne Cot Memorial.
Panel 28A.

Born in Battersea, southwest London on 22 July 1893, John Wellard was the sixth child of Henry Wellard and his wife, Emily (nee Heavens). He was baptised on 14 February 1894 at St Bartholomew's Church in Battersea. Home at the time was 104, Tyneham Road, Battersea. Henry, a carpenter, later registered his youngest child for school on 18 April 1898 at Holden Street School.

After this time, no details have been located about John's life until 1911. Before this, despite extensive searches, nothing has been revealed of the family's whereabouts, including any information from the 1901 Census. Elements of the family appear later, in the 1911 Census, with Emily living with two of her children, Bessie and Harold, at 26, Hanbury Road, Battersea. However, John was living separately from his family at that point and boarding with Isaac and Helen Smith and their three children at 12, Richardson Road, Hove in Kent. Both Isaac and John, then 17, are listed as boot repairers, with John being Isaac's assistant.

John enlisted at Chichester in the period following 9 October 1916, initially joining The Buffs and later being allocated the service number 203249 during the renumbering of TF Infantry in 1917. This would confirm that John was with 4th Bn The Buffs around the spring of 1917. However, at first sight, this does not explain why he then retained a five-figure service number, 34000, at the time he transferred over to the 1/7 Royal Warwicks. Though, given how batches of new service numbers were allocated to regiments, the likely answer seems to be that his six-figure number issued by The Buffs would likely be a duplicate of a number already issued to a soldier in the Royal Warwicks. He has therefore likely reverted to the number he was allocated on enlistment in order to avoid any administrative confusion at Regimental Headquarters in Warwick.

John died on 8 October 1917. It would appear that having initially been wounded in action, he was then reported as missing and subsequently presumed dead. He nominated his mother, Emily, to receive his effects and she received his savings of £2.15/6d and a war gratuity of £3.00. Emily also received a dependant's pension of 12/6d a week.

With no known grave, John is commemorated on the memorial wall at Tyne Cot Cemetery. It is not known if he is commemorated on any memorials locally.

Sydney John Willis – Private 268279

Killed in action on 8 October 1917, aged 26 years.
Commemorated at Tyne Cot Memorial.
Panel 28A.

Sydney Willis was the second of five children born to coachman and groom James Willis and his wife, Edith (nee Bramham). He was born in October of 1891 in the South Yorkshire city of Sheffield.

In the 1901 Census, nine-year-old Sydney is listed as living with his parents and ten-year-old brother, Charles. The census also records three younger sisters: Edith, eight, Jessie, seven, and Norah, five. Jessie subsequently passed away in January 1903. Home for the family at that time was 81, Penistone Road, in what is now the Wadsley Bridge area of the city.

By the time of the 1911 Census, the family had moved to a six-roomed house at 112, Wicker, in central Sheffield. Sydney had turned 19 and was working as a furnace hand for one of the city's many steel manufacturers. Though still working with horses, his father, James, was also in the employ of one of the local steel mills and working as a groom. Brother Charles was working as a clerk for a paper merchant and youngest sister, Norah, was 15 and still at school. Edith is believed to have left home to marry and marriage would not be so far off for Sydney either. He subsequently married Alice Nowell, at Sheffield on 1 June 1914.

At the time Sydney enlisted at Sheffield, on 9 December 1915, the couple were living at 36, Leavy Greave Road, in the Broomhill area of Sheffield. By then, Sydney was working as a travelling mineral water seller. Having signed up as Private 3884 Willis of the West Riding Divisional Royal Engineers, a territorial unit, he was initially posted to the army reserve. His medical notes describe him as 24 years and two months old, standing at 5′ 4½″ tall. He had a 37″ chest with a 3″ expansion. Scars were noted on the left side of his chest, above his right eye and on the back of his neck.

After remaining with the reserves, Sydney was subsequently transferred to serve with the 96th Training Reserve Battalion. He was then transferred again, this time to the 11th Bn, Royal Warwicks, which he joined in France on Christmas Eve, 1916. However, Sydney would not remain with the unit for long and on 13 January 1917 he was transferred to the 1/7 Royal Warwicks, which were undergoing a month of training at Warloy, France. Sydney was subsequently reported as missing, presumed dead, on 8 October 1917.

As his widow, Alice received her husband's savings of £9.14/3d, along with a war gratuity of £6.10/-. She was also awarded a dependant's pension of 13/9d a week. Alice later remarried, taking the surname of Hague, and moved to 70, Cambridge Street, Rotherham.

With no known grave, Sydney is commemorated on the memorial wall at Tyne Cot. It is not known if he is commemorated on any local memorials.

Chapter 7

Druid: The Story of a Tank

Though not mentioned in either the battalion war diaries for the 1/5, 1/6 or 1/7 Royal Warwicks, or the war diary for the 143rd Infantry Brigade, the infantry attack of 4 October 1917 was actually supported by tanks. Their deployment was successful overall and offered effective armoured support to those infantry units involved in the attack. However, the part that they actually played in assisting the 1/7 Royal Warwicks to achieve their objectives at the opening of the battle is somewhat limited.

Before the attack commenced, a total of twelve tanks had assembled around a day before and waited under special, brick rubble camouflage pattern nets for the advance. The tanks, all Mark IV types, were from No.10 Coy, D Battalion of the 1st Brigade, The Tank Corps. They had been divided into three sections, comprising four tanks each, and their overall objective was to assist the attacking infantry battalions in securing the capture of various strongpoints and strategic locations, in and around the village of Poelcapelle.

By the time the attack was due to commence, at 0600 hours, eleven of the twelve tanks had already moved into position on the St Julien/Poelcapelle Road, waiting ahead of the attacking infantry. Commanded by Lieutenant TK Cook and originally part of 3 Section, the twelfth tank, D11, named 'Dominie', had withdrawn with mechanical problems. When the attack commenced, 1 Section, comprising tanks D1 'Druid', D2 'Duke of Cornwall, D3 'Drone' and D13 'Dame', turned southeast and headed for their objectives.

Druid and Dame were both female variants. That is to say that each of them was armed with five Lewis Guns each, as opposed to the male variants, which were equipped instead with two 6 pdr guns, as well as three Lewis Guns. The going was difficult for the tanks, which initially had to negotiate a shattered road surface and fallen trees on the main road, before traversing difficult ground across the heavily shelled fields.

Peeling off to support the attack on Terrier Farm, both tanks had been very effective in their advance up to that point. However, after the fall of Gloster Farm, another German strongpoint, the infantry was very quickly able to over-run Terrier Farm. Therefore, by the time Dame and Druid had arrived, there was little for them to do. Consequently, with no further assistance to the infantry required, the tanks withdrew.

Druid, commanded by Lieutenant D.J. Salmon, headed back up onto the St Julien/Poelcapelle Road, with the intention of making for base. However, as they pushed for home, they identified a sniper in a blockhouse who was 'harassing' the infantry. Druid engaged the blockhouse with machine-gun fire, but in the process of doing so, the tank slid off the ruined road surface and ended up stuck in a drainage ditch. German artillery soon spotted the helpless tank and fired upon it as the crew struggled in vain with the unditching beam. Though most of the crew managed to escape unharmed, Lieutenant Salmon was wounded and one crewman, Sergeant Frederick Procter, was killed. The relevant war diary entry for Tank Corps HQ noted:

> *Those were the only casualties suffered to personnel during the day and the tank in question had, up until then, been one of the lucky ones, having enjoyed excellent targets and killed a considerable number of the enemy.*

Although Frederick Procter was not serving with the 1/7 Royal Warwicks at the time he was killed, his death is directly and inextricably linked to the advance of that infantry unit on the day. Moreover, he is the only man from his unit to have been killed while providing that armoured support. As such, it is right that his remarkable story should be told alongside those of the men he supported that day and who also did not survive the action.

Mk IV female tank 'Druid' ditched at the side of the St Julien/Poelcapelle Road. The photo was taken around a year after the war ended. Note the pile of unexploded shells at the base of the first tree on the right. (*Public domain*)

Sergeant Frederick 'Fred' Procter. Seen here while in service with the City of London (Roughriders) Imperial Yeomanry. (*Public domain*)

Born in London on 25 January 1884, he was one of six children born to printer and stationer John Procter and his wife, Susannah. Frederick, or Fred, as he was known, worked as a bank clerk for the London and South Western Bank. However, he also had an interest in the military and joined the City of London (Roughriders) Imperial Yeomanry on 20 March 1908, as Trooper 1311 Proctor. This was just before the creation of the TF under the Haldane reforms. His address at the time was 21, Helier Gardens, Brixton, London.

The 1911 Census has Fred, his mother and three of his siblings living at 75, Trinity Street, Lambeth. Though, by the time of the census, his father had passed away. The same year, Fred married Alice Hodges in Lambeth.

Fred remained with the Roughriders at the outbreak of war and achieved the rank of sergeant on 5 October 1914. However, in March 1915, he was discharged and promptly joined the Royal Navy. Issued with the service number F3487, Fred was described in his naval records as being 5′ 8½″ tall, with a 35″ chest. He had brown hair, hazel eyes and a fresh complexion. Posted to HMS *President II* for land operations, Fred crewed armoured cars and is believed to have served in the Dardanelles. (Gallipoli campaign.) However, he subsequently left the navy and rejoined the army with the service number

2939 and initially served in the Machine Gun Corps (MGC), where he later went on to be awarded the MM. Though little detail is known, there is a short citation, which reads:

[Fred] Set a fine example of coolness and courage under heavy fire and indicating targets on April 9, 1917, during the attack on Neuville Vitasse.

He later transferred to the Tank Corps and was issued with the service number 200822, serving with D Company, until he was killed in action. After his death, his wife, Alice, received his savings of £1.16/8d and a war gratuity of £21.10/-. She was also awarded a dependant's pension of 34/7d a week.

Fred's body was never recovered from the battlefield and he is therefore commemorated on the memorial wall at Tyne Cot on Panel 159. It is not known if he is commemorated on any local war memorials.

Chapter 8

After the Guns

After being withdrawn from the Western Front on 21 November 1917, the 1/7 Royal Warwicks spent the rest of the war in the mountains around the Val D'Assa region of Northern Italy. They fought on the Asiago Plateau and at the Battle of Vittoria Veneto and by the time the Armistice was signed, they had withdrawn to the town of Granezza. In early 1919, with no further need for their presence, the battalion was finally sent home, after four years of active service.

It is well documented that life for many returning soldiers was difficult. Especially in terms of finding work. Many found that the 'land fit for heroes' that they were promised by Prime Minister David Lloyd George simply did not exist. The 1921 Census shows that, for Joe Waite too, life in Coventry soon after the war held its own challenges. At that time, as with many of the returning veterans, the then 22-year-old Joe was out of work. Though it does seem he had previously been employed as a driller by the firm Swifts, sometime after being demobbed.

Home by then was once more 18, Cow Lane, the dilapidated old street in the city centre from where Joe had most likely left to go to war. He was living there under the same roof as his father, Joe Snr, who having been previously employed as an iron turner at the Maudslay Motor Company, was also unemployed. Resident too was young Joe's stepmother, Maud, and his 17-year-old sister, Laura, who was working as a linker for a firm called Quinton Hosiery. Present too was his brother, George, who at 14 was employed as an errand boy for a firm of clothiers in the nearby High Street. His sister, Ethel, had by this time been sent to the US and initially worked in service for a family in Detroit, Michigan. She was just 11 years old when she left Coventry in 1913, but remained in America, eventually starting a new life and family of her own.

However, for Joe, his fortunes would eventually turn and in July 1926, he married Ada Florence Arch. Just over three years later, in October 1929, their first and only child, Margaret Ethel, was born. Home for the family was 16, Batemans Acre, a modest end-of-terrace house, which still stands today and is located in the Coundon area of the city.

Joe's father had eventually moved out of Cow Lane too and had made a home with Maud in a small, terraced house at 92, Mulliner Street, Foleshill.

Not far from where Maud's family, the Sidwells, kept their pub, The Bricklayers Arms, in neighbouring Cromwell Street. It was at the Mulliner Street address, on 3 August 1933, that Joe Waite Snr passed away, aged 55 years. He was subsequently laid to rest in London Road Cemetery.

Life for young Joe and his family would have been pleasant enough. They were living a comfortable suburban existence in a nice neighbourhood and Joe had eventually been promoted to a works engineer foreman at the nearby Standard Motor Co factory. However, in 1939, war with Germany loomed once more and by 1940 the city had, due to its massive manufacturing capability, become a prime target for German bombers. Indeed, the Standard itself quickly switched to war production and began to manufacture anything from armoured cars to aircraft. Perhaps one of its most famous products was the De Haviland Mosquito. A revolutionary design for its time, this formidably successful twin-engine fighter-bomber was nicknamed the Wooden Wonder, owing to the fact that much of its structure was formed of lightweight plywood.

On the night of 14 November 1940, the city was devastated in a night of intense bombing that would later become known as the Coventry Blitz. This deadly raid would become the one most commonly referred to in the context of the city's collective wartime experience. Nevertheless, there was a second large raid, often referred to as the Easter Blitz, which took place over the nights of the weekend of 8 to 10 April 1941. It was this raid that must have made Joe feel that his old enemy had returned to torment him once more.

Coventry citizens make their way through bomb damage seen from Jordan Well, towards the city centre. The Council House clock tower is seen to the left while to the right is the spire of the burned-out St Michael's Cathedral. The spire of Holy Trinity is furthest right. (*Author's collection*)

On the night of the ninth, Joe had already left to work a night shift at the Standard, leaving Ada and Margaret at home. Though he could not have known it, the two most precious people in his life would not survive the night.

Though not a direct hit on the house, a bomb detonated very close by and damaged a number of houses in Bateman's Acre. Number 16 was extensively damaged, with its roof blown off and its timbers badly damaged. The blast had cracked the walls and taken the plaster off, the force of the blast likely killing Ada and Margaret instantly and burying them under the rubble. Margaret's body was recovered the next day, on the tenth, and her mother's body was recovered the day after that. Ada was 42 years

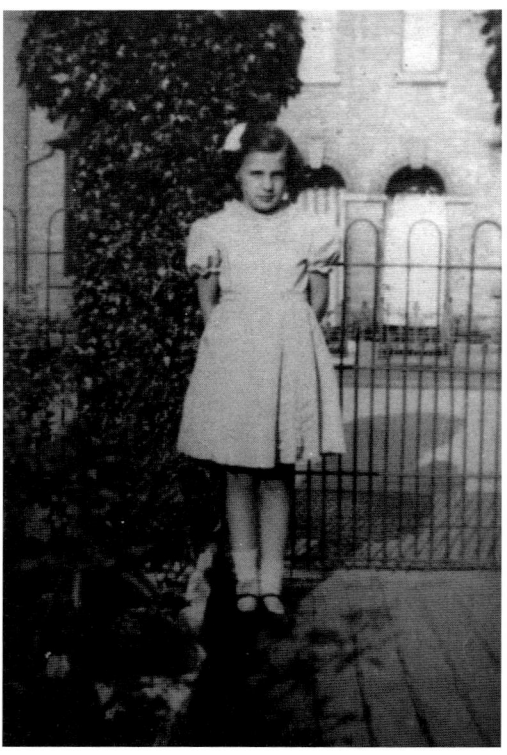

Margaret 'Babs' Waite. (*Photo – Waite family archive*)

old and her daughter was just 11. The cause of death for both was recorded simply as 'due to war operations'.

Once again, Joe's name would appear in the Midland Daily Telegraph, though this time for the most tragic of reasons, as he posted an obituary for his lost family on 14 April.

Waite – Ada Florence (Biddy). Dearly loved wife of Joe: also Margaret Ethel (Babs), beloved daughter, 16 Bateman's Acre, Coventry. Passed away April 9.

Both Biddy and Babs were laid to rest in the communal grave at London Road Cemetery. This was established for those citizens of Coventry who lost their lives during the German air raids on the city.

In order to avoid, as much as possible, housing shortages caused by enemy raids, many bomb-damaged properties were quickly repaired and reoccupied. In terms of 16, Bateman's Acre, not only did the local authority decide that the property would be repaired, but Joe also made the extraordinary decision that he would continue to live there. He did so, for the rest of his life. Though, in the

The memorial wall at London Road Cemetery, which holds the names of over 800 victims of the bombing raids on Coventry and who rest nearby. (*Author's photo*)

years that followed, on the coat rack in the hallway of that house, Margaret's school hat and coat always hung.

For Joe, life went on without his beloved Biddy and Babs and he remained close to his family. Though, it seems that there was always a distance between him and his stepmother, Maud. My mother recalled that he would always come around for the family Christmas dinner and loved to be around the kids. However, he seldom had much to say to Maud on such occasions and often left early. Maud subsequently passed away, aged 64, in the June of 1954 and was laid to rest with her husband.

The year after Maud died, the Coventry Evening Telegraph for 17 March 1955 carried a report for a forthcoming reunion dinner for men of the 7th Bn Royal Warwicks who had served in the Great War. It was to be held at the Queen Victoria Road Drill Hall on Saturday, 26 March. This report covered the fortieth anniversary of the men being mobilised for war and shed just a further small chink of light on Joe's service.

He featured quite significantly in the article and was named as being only one of two 16-year-old soldiers

Photo of Maud Waite, probably taken around the mid-1930s. (*Photo – Waite family archive*)

who were not discovered as being underage and sent back to England. The other was his lifelong friend, George West. It appears that both Joe and George struck up a close bond while serving and regularly enjoyed friendly banter about who was the youngest of the two to land in France. The surviving records settle the argument by proving that George was on the SS *Copenhagen* when the battalion originally sailed for France in March 1915. Joe, it is now clear, did not sail until the following June, meaning that George landed first. However, Joe had the drop on George in terms of age, as he was six months younger than George so could still retain bragging rights for being the youngest of the two.

In the years after their service, both of them played rugger together and also enjoyed the odd game of darts. And, as with so many men who forged bonds in the hardest of times, they enjoyed an enduring friendship.

Intriguingly, the article also mentions that, while in France, Joe had seen an enemy counterattack beginning to form against their positions. He raised the alarm and was therefore instrumental in instigating the British artillery bombardment that 'smashed' the assault. Unfortunately, no direct mention of this could be found in the battalion war diary and the exact circumstances therefore remain a mystery.

The article also reported on the fact that he had worked at the Standard Motor Co for thirty years and was at the factory when Biddy and Babs were killed in the air raid. It went on to report that although he was not bitter, he was less inclined to talk so cheerfully about his wartime experiences than some of his old comrades.

The wedding of Geoff Waite to Elaine Liggins. Joe Waite is on the far left of the party. (*Photo – Waite family archive*)

In January 1968, his nephew, Geoff, the son of his brother, George, married Elaine Liggins. The wedding party was of course captured in a photograph and this is likely the last known photo taken of Joe. He can be seen at the far left of the group, smiling broadly, as the good-humoured and well-liked man that he was. His brother, George, can be seen around four people to the left of the bride and the small boy standing to the front of George is Joe's great-nephew and the author of this work.

After George died, just a year after the wedding, we still used to visit Uncle Joe regularly at home in Bateman's Acre and I remember that he used to have a small blue budgie, Billy, as a companion. Joe would often pop around to his local pub, The Holyhead, for a drink, but Billy was always left with the TV on so he didn't get lonely. I remember too, the school hat and coat that used to hang in the hall. Though there was never any mention I can recall of what happened to the little girl who used to wear them. It was only many years later that I found out the sad truth of the tragic events of that night in 1941.

Joe's remarkable life came to an end on 4 November 1973, at the age of 75. He passed away in Whitley Hospital, Coventry, having suffered a heart attack, likely brought about as a result of the acute chest infection he was suffering from at the time. His funeral took place at Canley Crematorium, where his

Joe Waite's headstone in Canley Crematorium. The 'MM' and engraved Royal Warwickshire cap badge are later additions to the original inscription. The photo was taken after the laying of the floral tribute, exactly 100 years after the action for which he was awarded his Military Medal. (*Author's photo*)

ashes rest today. When he was cremated, his beloved Babs's school hat was placed in the coffin with him.

Like his own story, those of the men who served with Joe are all now a part of history. His old friend, George West, survived Joe by many years. Passing away in June 1992 at the age of 94, George must surely have been one of the very last, if not sole surviving soldier from the 1/7 Royal Warwicks who fought at the Battle of Broodseinde. If such is the case, his passing finally wiped from living memory the last mental images of the men who fell, the survivors and the experiences they shared during the three days they held their ground in the blood-soaked mud of Flanders.

As has already been acknowledged, there remains not one person alive who served in the Great War. As such, we, the generations who came afterward and who owe them so much, should rightly ensure that their memory lives on. After all, the chief purpose of this book is to do just that. And though the stories of just a few men are told here, at least it can be said that, in some small way, the lives of these men, who are perhaps only remembered by their families, or are already lost to living memory, can be celebrated once more.

For me, finding the words to close a book like this kept me thinking for quite some time. Though, in the end, I could never quite produce something that I felt worked. But then I realised that I didn't have to. Instead, I understood that the words should come from the hearts of that generation themselves. And in that regard, one of the most powerful mediums they used to describe their world was poetry.

Having opened this book with arguably the most famous poem about the fighting in Flanders, it is a less well-known poem, written in 1914 by F Chatterton Hennequin and Phylis Norman Parker, that I have chosen to close with. Unlike the work of many of the better-known war poets, such as Siegfried Sassoon, Wilfred Owen and Rupert Brooke, I felt that this perfectly conveyed the humour, the character, the comradeship and the great bond of friendship that many common soldiers experienced. That was a view amply enforced when I saw a video of the poem recited by Ted Francis of Birmingham, a Great War veteran, and an old Royal Warwick. Delivering the monologue in an unmistakable Brummie accent, it held great resonance for me as a proud Midlander. It was also plain to see how much the words meant to him. Especially when it was clear that, even after all that time, the memories it evoked could still bring him to tears. I'll therefore leave the truly wonderful 'Spotty' to allow that extraordinary generation to have the last word.

SPOTTY

By F. Chatterton Hennequin & Phyllis Norman Parker (1914)

Spotty was my chum, he was, a ginger-headed bloke,
An everlasting gas-bag and as stubborn as a moke.
He give us all the 'ump he did before it come to war,
By sportin' all 'is bits of French, what no-one asked him for.

He says to me, 'Old Son,' he says, 'you won't have 'arf a chance,
When I gets in conversation with them demerselles of France.'
I says to 'im, 'You close yer face,' he says, 'All right bong swore,'
Don't 'urt yourself mong sher amy,' then 'so long! oh re-vore!'

When we got our marching orders you can bet we wasn't slow,
A-singing, 'Tipperary! it's a long, long way to go.'
On the transport 'ow he swanked it, with 'is parley vooing airs,
Till I nearly knocked 'is 'ead off 'cos he said I'd 'mal de mares'.

When we landed, what a beano, how them Frenchies laughed and cried,
And I see old Spotty swelling fit to bust 'iself with pride,
He was blowin' of 'em kisses and was singing, 'Vive la France,'
Till the Sergeant-Major copped 'im, then he says, 'Kel mauvay chance!'

But we didn't get no waitin', where we went nobody knows,
And it wasn't like the fighting that you see in picture shows.
We 'ad days of 'ell together, till they told us to retire,
And then Spotty's flow of language set the water carts on fire.

'Im and me was very lucky, for two-thirds of us was dead,
With their greasy 'black Marias' and the shrapnel overhead.
And every time they missed us when the fire was murderous 'ot,
Old Spotty says, 'Honcore! Honcore!' that's French for 'Rotten shot.'

And then at last there came the time, we got 'em on the go,
And 'im and me was fightin' at a little place called Mo (Meaux)
A-lying down together in a 'ole dug with our 'ands
For you gets it quick and sudden if you moves about or stands,

We was sharing 'arf a'fag we was, Yus! turn and turnabout,
When I felt 'im move towards me, and he ses, 'Oh mate I'm out.'

'Is eyes they couldn't see me – they never will no more,
But 'is twisted mouth it whispered, 'So long matey, Oh Re-vore!'

There was no one quite the same to me, for 'im and me was pals
And if I could 'ave 'im wiv me you could keep your fancy gals
But he's talking French in 'eaven, and it's no good feelin' sore
But Gawd knows 'ow I miss 'im, 'So long Spotty, Oh Revore!'

List of Chief Information Sources

(Not Exhaustive)

Organisations:
2 Explore Flanders Fields
Commonwealth War Graves Commission
Coventry City Council
Coventry Evening Telegraph
Herbert Art Gallery and Museum, Coventry
In Flanders Fields Museum, Belgium
National Archives of Australia & Australian War Memorial
Passchendaele Memorial Museum, 1917. Belgium
The Coventry Society
The Imperial War Museum
The Ministry of Defence
The National Archives
The National Army Museum
The National Library of Scotland
The Royal Regiment of Fusiliers Museum, (Royal Warwickshire Regt), Warwick.
The Western Front Association

(This list also acknowledges all of those individuals and organisations, private, commercial and religious, who currently maintain national and local memorials to the fallen but are too numerous to mention here.)

Web Resources:

A Street Near You
https://astreetnearyou.org

Ancestry.co.uk
www.ancestry.co.uk

British Newspaper Archive
www.britishnewspaperarchive.co.uk

Family Researcher – Dictionary of Old Occupations
www.familyresearcher.co.uk

Find My Past
www.findmypast.co.uk

Forces War Records
www.forces-war-records.co.uk

Free BMD
www.freebmd.org.uk

Great War Forum
www.greatwarforum.org

Hero in my Street
hero-inmystreet.com

Lives of the First World War
https://livesofthefirstworldwar.iwm.org.uk

London War Memorial Records
https://londonwarmemorial.co.uk

Nuneaton and North Warwickshire Family History Society
https://nanwfhs.org.uk

Roll of Honour
www.roll-of-honour.com

Tank Poelcapelle
https://tankpoelcapelle.be

The Funk Hole
www.thefunkhole.co.uk

The London Gazette
www.thegazette.co.uk

The Long, Long Trail
www.longlongtrail.co.uk

Traces of War
www.tracesofwar.com

Visit Flanders
www.visitflanders.com

War Gratuity – Resources in WW1 Records
https://wargratuity.uk

The Wartime Memories Project
www.wartimememoriesproject.com

Wikipedia
www.wikipedia.org

Index of Fallen Soldiers

Index